Isaiah 26:3–4
"PERFECT PEACE XV"

11:29

VANESSA RAYNER

authorHOUSE®

AuthorHouse™
1663 Liberty Drive
Bloomington, IN 47403
www.authorhouse.com
Phone: 1 (800) 839-8640

Published by AuthorHouse 07/25/2018

ISBN: 978-1-5462-5225-2 (sc)
ISBN: 978-1-5462-5224-5 (e)

Library of Congress Control Number: 2018908746

Print information available on the last page.

Contents

A Gift . . .

*P*resented to

_____

*F*rom

_____

*D*ate

_____

The Individuals who hear God's voice best . . .
Are the Individuals who know his word most.

Theme

The message of **Isaiah 26:3-4** is "Perfect Peace." This is the distinct and unifying composition of this book with the subtitle **11:29**.

A Song of Praise

You will keep in perfect peace all who trust in
you, all whose thoughts are fixed on you!
Trust in the Lord always, for the Lord
God is the eternal Rock.
Isaiah 26:3-4 NLT

PS: Isaiah 26 has 21 verses, and is considered "A Song of Praise."

Prayer

Oh, Heavenly Father,
I thank you for another opportunity
to write another book.
I pray that your people are prospering
daily in their spirit, soul,
and body by reading, Perfect Peace Books.

Oh, Heavenly Father,
I ask in Jesus' name that the Holy Spirit will
help readers to remember Your word.
I pray it will give them peace, and joy,
especially when they need it the most.
I thank You for blessing those that
help Your work go forth.

Oh, Heavenly Father,
You have made it clear that You will reward
those that bless your servant.
It could be through prayer, words of encouragement,
to giving that person a cup of water.

Oh, Heavenly Father,
I give you all the Glory, Honor and Praise in Jesus' name.

Amen.

Author's Notes

Author notes generally provide a way to add extra information to one's book that may be awkward and inappropriate to include in the text of the book itself. It offers supplemental contextual details on the aspects of the book. It can help readers understand the book content and the background details of the book better. The times and dates of researching, reading, and gathering this information are not included; mostly when I typed on it.

1744; Monday, 09 April 2018; Started on book XV.

2149; Saturday, 14 April 2018

1722; Wednesday, 18 April 2018

1925; Thursday, 19 April 2018

0632; Sunday, 22 April 2018

1539; Sunday, 29 April 2018

1638; Thursday, 03 May 2018; Just finished emailing the approval for the book cover concerning Isaiah 26:3-4 "Perfect Peace XIV" G-Men. Praise God!

0628; Friday, 04 May 2018; I'm going to work on the book about an hour before I leave to go to work.

0138; Sunday, 06 May 2018

1906; Friday, 11 May 2018

1208; Saturday, 12 May 2018

1026; Sunday, 13 May 2018; My sister (Regina) from Texas, and her daughter, my niece (Dalshundria) from Memphis, just left for San Francisco for my niece new job with Sprint. We did a selfie before they left; I'm not photogenic at all, LOL. (I might put it in the back of the book, I have several months to think about it.)

1906; Wednesday, 16 May 2018

1419; Saturday, 19 May 2018

0642; Sunday, 20 May 2018; Enjoying Apostle D. Smith visit from Sikeston, Mo. We going to drive to Starkville, Ms to Bishop Glenda Coleman's birthday dinner at her church that starts at 1:30 pm. Father, we are asking for traveling grace, today. Praise God!

1932; Monday, 21 May 2018

1723; Tuesday, 22 May 2018

1912; Wednesday, 23 May 2018

1828; Friday, 25 May 2018

0506; Saturday, 26 May 2018

0706; Sunday, 27 May 2018

1046; Monday, 28 May 2018; Memorial Day

1729; Thursday, 31 May 2018

2141; Friday, 01 June 2018

0739; Saturday, 02 June 2018

1824; Monday, 04 June 2018

1049; Tuesday, 05 June 2018

1907; Wednesday, 06 June 2018

0612; Thursday, 07 June 2018

1639; Friday, 08 June 2018

0647; Saturday, 09 June 2018

0713; Sunday, 10 June 2018

1758; Monday, 11 June 2018

0523; Tuesday, 12 June 2018; Under the weather, today. Praise God, anyhow.

0000; Wednesday, 13 June 2018

0002; Thursday, 14 June 2018; The pain in wrist/hand will not let me sleep. I guess I'll work on a paragraph or two until my Rx kicks in. Oh, Heavenly Father, just one touch from You . . .AD Moore, Happy Birthday Bro!

1155; Friday, 15 June 2018

0630; Sunday, 17 June 2018

0000; Monday, 18 June 2018

0005; Tuesday, 19 June 2018

0000; Wednesday, 20 June 2018

1722; Thursday, 21 June 2018

0000; Friday, 22 June 2018

0000; Saturday, 23 June 2018

0550; Sunday, 24 June 2018

1641; Monday, 25 June 2018

1756; Tuesday, 26 June 2018

1924; Wednesday, 27 June 2018

1630; Thursday, 28 June 2018

0000; Friday, 29 June 2018

0618; Saturday, 30 June 2018

0621; Sunday, 01 July 2018

1620; Monday, 02 July 2018

0635; Tuesday, 03 July 2018

0405; Wednesday, 04 July 2018; Happy 4th of July

1428; Thursday, 05 July 2018

0828; Friday, 06 July 2018; I'm going to "tap" on this book a little before I travel to Little Rock to my oldest sister, Easter's house. My brother, AD, and his wife, Rose are going to stop by her home on their way back to Chicago from Biloxi, MS.

0716; Saturday, 07 July 2018

0000; Sunday, 08 July 2018

1645; Monday, 09 July 2018; Oldest Son Birthday, Alvin. L. Jackson. Pray Father Bless You with Many Mooooooore!

0858; Saturday, 14 July 2018; A thought dropped in my spirit to add to Author's Closing Remarks while I was working on Isaiah 26:3-4 "Perfect Peace XVI." Praise God! Saints. **P.S.:** I'm still praying over "Perfect Peace XV" to the Lord God Almighty.

2243; Wednesday, 18 July 2018

1218; Thursday, 19 July 2018; Happy Birthday "Mom" ~ Ulyer Moore ~ RIP

Peace is given only to those whose mind and heart reclines upon the LORD. God's peace is increased in us according to the knowledge of His Holy Word.

> **Grace and peace be multiplied unto you**
> **through the knowledge of God,**
> **and of Jesus our LORD.**
> *2* Peter 1:2 KJV

Thanks . . . To the Readers of the world

As a disciple of the LORD Jesus Christ, I have learned true success comes when we are seeking and striving to do God's purpose for our lives. Our real happiness lies in doing God's will; not in fame and fortune.

I appreciate your support. Thanks for helping me spread "Perfect Peace" through your e-mail, Facebook, Twitter, LinkedIn, Instagram, Tumblr, Messenger and or other accounts to your family, friends, neighbors, co-workers, church family, internet social friends, and associates.

Remember, you may not know until you get to heaven just how much a song you sung, kind words spoken by you or even a book you suggested reading, at the right moment, encourage a person to keep on going when a few minutes before they were tempted to give up on life and their walk with the LORD.

I greatly appreciate your love and kindness to this ministry.

Acknowledgements

First and foremost, I wish to express my sincere gratitude to ***"Our Heavenly Father"*** for his guidance, patience, mercy, and lovingkindness throughout the writing of this book.

Introduction

For Those Who Want to Be Kept In "Perfect Peace"

This book was prepared and written to open your mind to a "Perfect Peace" that comes only from God. I'm striving to elevate you into a "Unique and Profound" awareness of God's presence around you at all time.

According to some people, it's hard to keep your mind on the LORD. While most Christians will agree that if you keep your mind stayed on the LORD, He will keep you in "Perfect Peace." This is why so many people enjoy going to church on Sundays and attending midweek services for peace and joy that they receive, but only for a short time.

You can experience the peace of the LORD throughout the day and every day. His unspeakable joy, his strength, his "Perfect Peace" in the midst of the storm whether it's at work, home, college, school, etc. You can also experience this peace, even when your day is going well.

This concept of this book was placed in my spirit by our Father, which art in heaven, to help me when he allowed Satan to test me at my workplace until he finished molding me into a MAP; (Minister/Ambassador/Pastor).

Throughout these pages, I will be focussing on biblical events, and facts surrounding the term "11:29." However, I am sure much more can be said concerning the term "11:29" in the Bible, so these subjects serve merely as an introduction and are not exhaustive by any means.

Dedication

This book is dedicated to . . .
I. The Three Branches of American Criminal Justice System

    A. Law Enforcement Agencies
1. Patrol Officers/Police Officers
2. Sheriffs
3. Deputies
4. Federal Agents
5. Game and Park Rangers
6. Detectives

    B. The Courts
1. Judges
2. Prosecutors
3. Defense Lawyers
4. Attorneys
5. Public Defenders
6. Jury Members

    C. Corrections
1. Probation Officers
2. Parole Officers
3. Corrections Officers

II. The Support Personnel of the American Criminal Justice System

    A. Record Clerks
    B. Receptionists
    C. Secretaries

III. Finally, with my Sincere Gratitude

    A. Attorney Gregory C. Krog, Jr.
    B. The Honorable Judge Louis J. Montesi, Jr., Division 13
    C. The Honorable Judge S. Ronald Lucchesi, Division 12

Chapter 1

NUMBERED
VERSES

The Bible as we know today was not originally written in English, Spanish, French, or any other modern language. The Bible has been translated into many languages from the biblical languages of Hebrew, Aramaic, and Greek. The Old Testament was written primarily in Hebrew with small parts being written in Aramaic, while the New Testament was originally written in Greek.

How we got the Bible translated in its present form started thousands of years ago. The first written Word of God was spoken to Moses on Mount Sinai and then chisel out on two stone tablets about 1400 BC. They are called "The Ten Commandments."

The time from 1400 BC to 1400 AD is called the Pre-Reformation History of the Bible. It covers the bringing forth of the scripture from the original languages and the 1,000 years of the Dark and Middle Ages when the Word of God was translated only in Latin. In the Middle Ages, the Catholic Church forbids the reading of the Bible by its congregation. They feared the people would misinterpret the texts. As a result, only the Church fathers had the right to make interpretations for its people.

The first hand-written English language Bible manuscripts were produced in 1380 AD by John Wycliffe. He was called the "Morning Star of Reformation." He was an Oxford professor, scholar, and theologian. He was well-known throughout Europe for his opposition to the teaching of the organized Church. John Wycliffe produced dozens of English language manuscript copies of the scriptures with the help of many faithful scribes.

The Pope was so mad by his translation of the Bible into English that 44 years after Wycliffe had died, he ordered his bones to be dug-up, crushed and scattered in the river. However, John Hus, one of John Wycliffe's followers continues to do the work that John Wycliffe started. Shortly, following the Council of Constance assembled, Hus was trialed and condemned. John Hus was burned at the stake July 6, 1415, with John Wycliffe's manuscript Bibles used as kindling for the fire. His last words were, "in 100 years, God will raise up a man whose calls for reform cannot be suppressed."

In 1519, almost a 100 years later, Martin Luther, nailed his famous 95 Theses of Contention into the church door at Wittenberg. The prophecy of John Hus became truth. John Wycliffe of England and John Hus of Bohemia are often called "Pre-reformers" by historians.

In the 1450's, Johann Gutenberg invented the 1st printing press, and the first book ever to be printed was a Latin Bible, printed in Mainz, Germany. His invention of mechanically movable parts started the printing revolution. The use of movable type was a vast improvement on the handwritten manuscripts, which was the existing method of book production. Legend has it that the idea came to him "like a ray of light."

Johann Gutenberg major work is the Gutenberg Bible also known as the 42-line Bible published in 1455. William Tyndale was a 16th-century Protestant reformer and scholar who, influenced by the work of Desiderius Erasmus and Martin Luther holds the importance of being the first English translator, to print the New Testament into the English language. In 1535 William Tyndale was arrested and jailed over a year, trialed for heresy and burned at the stake. Much of his work finally found its way in the King James Version of the Bible, published in 1611, the works of about 54 scholars.

Martin Luther had a small head-start on William Tyndale. Martin Luther declared his intolerance for the Roman Church's corruption on Halloween in 1517, by nailing his 95 Theses of Contention to the Wittenberg's church door. In the following months, he translates the New Testament into German from the 1516 Greek-Latin New Testament of Desiderius Erasmus. It was published September 1522. Luther also published a German Pentateuch in 1523. In the 1530's, he would go on to publish the entire Bible in German.

Myles Coverdale and John "Matthew Thomas" Rogers were devoted followers of William Tyndale and carried the

English Bible project forward. Myles Coverdale completed translating the Old Testament, and on October 4, 1535, printed the first complete Bible in the English language. It is known as the Coverdale Bible.

In 1539, Thomas Cranmer, the Archbishop of Canterbury, hired Myles Coverdale at the request of King Henry VIII to publish the "Great Bible." It began the first English Bible for public use. It was distributed to every church, chained to the pulpit, and a reader was even provided so that the illiterate could hear the Word of God in plain English. Cranmer's Bible published by Coverdale was known as the "Great Bible" due to its great size. Seven editions of this version were printed between April 1539 and December 1541.

It was not that King Henry VIII; the King of England had a change of conscience regarding publishing the Bible in English. His motives were more sinister, but the Lord sometimes uses the evil intentions of men to bring about His glory. King Henry VIII had requested that the Pope permit him to divorce his wife and marry his mistress. The Pope refused, King Henry VIII responded by marrying his mistress anyway, later having two of his many wives executed. King Henry VIII turned away from the Pope by renouncing Roman Catholicism. He then took England out from under Rome's religious control and declared himself as the reigning head of the new Church.

This new branch of the Christian Church became known as the Anglican Church or the Church of England. King Henry VIII acted essentially as its "Pope." His first act was to defy the wishes of Rome by funding the printing of the scriptures in English. This was the first authorized English Bible.

After King Henry VIII, King Edward VI took the throne, and after his death, the reign of Queen "Bloody" Mary was the next. She was the oldest daughter of King Henry VIII. Queen Mary desire was to return England back to the Roman Church.

Therefore, in 1555, John "Thomas Matthew" Rogers and Thomas Cranmer were both burned at the stake. Queen Mary went on to burn reformers at the stake by the hundreds for the crime of being a Protestant. This era was known as the Marian Exile, and the refugees fled from England.

In the 1550's, the Church at Geneva, Switzerland was very sympathetic to the reformer refugees and was one of only a few safe havens for a desperate people. These people frequently met in Geneva, Switzerland led by Myles Coverdale and John Foxe. John Foxe is the publisher of the famous Foxe's Book of Martyrs. It tells about the lives, sufferings and triumphant deaths of the early Christian and the Protestant Martyrs. The New Testament was completed in 1557, and the complete Bible was first published in 1560. It became known as the Geneva Bible.

The Geneva Bible was the first Bible to add numbered verses to the chapters so that referencing specific passages would be easier. The Geneva Bible is also considered the first English Study Bible. The Geneva Bible became the Bible of choice for over 100 years of English speaking Christians. The Bible itself retains over 90% of William Tyndale's original English translation. It was the first Bible taken to America and the Bible of the Puritans and Pilgrims.

The Roman Catholic Church lost the battle to suppress God's Holy Word. In 1582, the Church of Rome surrendered their fight for Latin only. They decided, if the Bible were to be available in English, they would at least have an Official Roman Catholic English Translation. The New Testament was translated at the Roman Catholic College in the city of Rheims. It was known as the Rheims New Testament. The Old Testament was translated by the Church of Rome in 1609 at the College in the city of Douay, and it was known as the Douay Old Testament. The combined product is commonly referred to as the Douay-Rheims Version.

The Protestant Bible and not just the Catholic Bibles had 80 books, not 66 until the1880's. They are called "The Apocrypha" which were books written hundreds of years before Christ. They were part of the Tyndale-Matthews Bible, the Great Bible, the Protestant Geneva Bible, and the King James Bible until their removal in the 1880's! Even, the original 1611 King James Bible contained the Apocrypha. King James threatened anyone who dares to print the Bible without the Apocrypha with heavy fines and a year in jail. Only for the last 120 years have the Protestant Church rejected these books and removed them from their Bibles.

Now in this day and age, translators of the Bible have taken various approaches in rendering it into English which ranges from "Formal Equivalence," to extreme use of "Dynamic Equivalence."

Note of Interests: If you like to know and read more about "Formal Equivalence" and "Dynamic Equivalence" read my book titled <u>Isaiah 26:3 – 4 "Perfect Peace" The Last Single Digit</u>.

~~~~~~~~~~~

Chapter 2

11ᵀᴴ CHAPTER, 29ᵀᴴ VERSE

The King James Bible has 66 books with 1,189 chapters. There are 39 books in the Old Testament and 27 in the New Testament. Bible scholars advanced studies revealed that the King James Bible also consist of 31,102 verses and 788,280 words.

The Old Testament of the Bible is the first part of the Christian Bible based upon a collection of ancient religious writings by the Israelites that are believed by most Christians and Jews to be the holy and sacred "Word of God." Scholars believe that the Old Testament was written by at least 23 authors beginning with Moses writing the 1ˢᵗ five books of the Bible and ending with the Prophet Malachi with the last book of the Old Testament named "Malachi."

The Old Testament has a total of 929 chapters, and many scholars believe it covers approximately 3600 years written over the course of 1070 years. Scholars believe about 400 years passed from the writing of the last book of the Old Testament to the writing of the birth of Christ in 2 BC recorded in the New Testament, Matthew 1. The New

Testament has 260 chapters and covers approximately 70 years, and it is considered the 2nd part of the Christian Bible.

In the Bible, 34 books have at least 11 chapters. However, out of the 34 books with the 11th chapters, many don't have the 29th verse. There are 13 books in the Old Testament, and only one book in the New Testament that contains the 11th chapter but no 29th verse.

The books of the Bible are listed below as they appear in the King James Bible, and those that are in parenthesis have less than 11 chapters. The books that are underlined have an 11th chapters, but no 29th verse. The number that is next to the book title is how many chapters in that particular book.

Old Testament:
The Books of the Law

1.	Genesis	50
2.	<u>Exodus</u>	<u>40</u>
3.	Leviticus	27
4.	Numbers	36
5.	Deuteronomy	34

Historical Books of the Bible

6.	<u>Joshua</u>	<u>24</u>
7.	Judges	21
8.	(Ruth)	4
9.	<u>1 Samuel</u>	<u>31</u>
10.	<u>2 Samuel</u>	<u>24</u>

<u>Poetry Books of the Bible</u>

<u>The Major Prophets Books of the Bible</u>

<u>The 12 Minor Prophets Books of the Bible</u>

31.	(Obadiah)	1
32.	(Jonah)	4
33.	(Micah)	7
34.	(Nahum)	3
35.	(Habakkuk)	3
36.	(Zephaniah)	3
37.	(Haggai)	2
38.	<u>Zechariah</u>	<u>14</u>
39.	(Malachi)	4

The New Testament has 27 books written by 8 different authors. Every author of the New Testament was Jewish, except Luke. Three of the writers were among the 12 disciples who walked and talked with Christ during his earthly ministry, and they were Matthew, Peter, and John. The other authors of the New Testament were Mark, Luke, Paul, James, Jude.

Note of Interests: John Mark known as Mark is the author of the Gospel of Mark. He was a believer in the early church, a cousin of Barnabas, and a traveling companion of Barnabas and Paul, Acts12:25. Luke was a physician and traveling companion of Paul on his 2nd missionary journey in Troas. Luke wrote the Gospel of Luke and the Book of Acts. Paul, previously known as Saul of Taurus, persecuted Christians, at first. He was converted and eventually wrote 13 books in the New Testament. James and Jude are half-brothers of Jesus Christ. James is mentioned a couple of times in the Bible, but at that time he was not a believer of Jesus Christ, John 7:2 – 5. James became a believer only after witnessing the resurrection of Jesus, 1 Corinthians 15:7. James eventually becomes a gracious leader, minister to the Jewish Christians, spoke at the Jerusalem Council, Acts 5:14 – 21. Jude too became a respected church leader. He warned Christians about false teachers who had infiltrated the church.

~~~~~~~~~~~~

New Testament
The Gospels

1.	Matthew	28
2.	Mark	16
3.	Luke	24
4.	John	21

The Acts of the Apostles

5.	Acts	28

Letters by Paul to the Churches

6.	Romans	16
7.	1 Corinthians	16
8.	2 Corinthians	13
9.	(Galatians)	6
10.	(Ephesians)	6
11.	(Philippians)	4
12.	(Colossians)	4

13.	(1 Thessalonians)	5
14.	(2 Thessalonians)	3

Letters by Paul to Individuals

15.	(1 Timothy)	6
16.	(2 Timothy)	4
17.	(Titus)	3
18.	(Philemon)	1

General Letters

19.	Hebrews	13
20.	(James)	5
21.	(1 Peter)	5
22.	(2 Peter)	3
23.	(1 John)	5
24.	(2 John)	1
25.	(3 John)	1
26.	(Jude)	1

Apocalypse of John

27.	Revelation	22

Note of Interests: Ephesians, Philippians, Colossians, and Philemon are referred to as "The Prison Epistles." These four epistles are in the New Testament were written by the Apostle Paul while he was under house arrest in Rome between 60 – 62 AD. Three of these prison letters were sent

13

to three of the churches Paul founded on his 2nd missionary journey, Acts 20:1 – 3. The 4th prison letter was written to Paul's friend and fellow laborer, Philemon, Philemon 1:1. It was a plea for forgiveness on behalf of Onesimus, Philemon runaway slave.

~~~~~~~~~~~

The Books of the Law

The Five Books of the Law are:
1. Genesis
2. Exodus
3. Leviticus
4. Numbers
5. Deuteronomy

They are also called:
1. Pentateuch
2. The Law
3. The Five Books of Moses
4. Torah

They were written by Moses, except for the account of Moses' death in Deuteronomy 34. Scholars believed Moses' successor, Joshua wrote that portion. Many scholars believe the Books of the Law were written between 1450 – 1410 BC on the east bank of the Jordan River before the Israelites entered the Land of Promise.

Chapter 3

GENESIS 11:29

And Abram and Nahor took them wives:
the name of Abram's wife was Sarai; and the name
of Nahor's wife, Milcah, the daughter of Haran,
the father of Milcah, and the father of Iscah.
Genesis 11:29 KJV

~~~

The Book of Genesis is the 1ˢᵗ book of the Old Testament and served as the 1ˢᵗ "Book of the Law" written by Moses. The word "Genesis" is taken from the Greek and signifies "the book of generation." The Book of Genesis can be divided into two sections which are called "Primeval History" and the "Ancestral History."

The Primeval History explains and gives details of God, the nature of his deity and his relationship with humanity in Genesis chapters 1 through 11. God created a world that was good and fit for mankind, but when man corrupted it with sin, God decided to destroy his creation, saving only righteous Noah to re-establish the relationship between man and God. The Primeval History covers approximately 2000 years. There are many ways to outline this section. A detailed outline is as follows:

Chapter 1 – 2	The Seven Days of Creation
Chapter 2	Adam and Eve
Chapter 3	The Fall
Chapter 4	Cain and Abel
Chapter 5	Genealogy of Adam to Noah
Chapter 6 – 9	The Great Flood
Chapter 10	The Table of Nations
Chapter 11	The Tower of Babel
Chapter 11	Genealogy of Shem to Abraham

The Ancestral History mentions the prehistory of Israel, God's chosen people in chapters 12 – 50. At God's command Noah's descendant Abraham journeys from his home into the land of Canaan, given to him by God, where he dwells as a sojourner, as does his son Isaac and his grandson Jacob. Jacob's name is changed to Israel, and through the intercession of his son, Joseph, the children of Israel descend into Egypt, a total of 70 people from their households, and God promises them a future of greatness. Genesis ends with Israel in Egypt, ready for the coming of Moses and the Exodus. The Ancestral History covers approximately 500 years between 2000 BC and 1500 BC. There are several ways to outline this section. A detail outline is listed below; ***hoping it arouse your attention to read it in its entirety.***

Abraham and Isaac

| Chapter 12 | God Chooses Abraham |
| Chapter 13 | Separation of Lot and Abraham |

Jacob

<u>Joseph</u>

The 11th chapter of Genesis begins with the biblical event surrounding the "Tower of Babel," verses 1 – 9. The next section of this chapter speaks on Shem's family line, verses 10 – 27. The last section of chapter 11, verses 27 – 32, mentions Abram's family, and this is where Genesis 11:29 is located, and it reads as follows:

<u>Genesis 11:29 KJV</u>

And Abram and Nahor took them wives: the name of Abram's wife was Sarai; and the name of Nahor's wife, Milcah, the daughter of Haran, the father of Milcah, and the father of Iscah.

<u>Genesis 11:29 NIV</u>

Abram and Nahor both married. The name of Abram's wife was Sarai, and the name of Nahor's wife was Milkah; she was the daughter of Haran, the father of both Milkah and Iskah.

When the above biblical event happened, it wasn't forbidden to marry a brother's daughter, until Leviticus 18:14. So Nahor married Haran's daughter named Milcah. Haran was Abram and Nahor's oldest brother. Scholars believed it was after his death when Nahor married his daughter.

Abram married Sarai, his half-sister, Genesis 20:12. Marriage between near relatives was allowed, but not marriage between individuals who had the same mother. Sarai was the daughter of Terah, the father of Abraham by another woman.

The life and legacy of Abram begin in Genesis 11. The Lord instructed Abram to leave his native country, relatives and go to a land he will show him. The Lord told Abram, He will make him a great nation. In Chapter 15 of Genesis, the Lord makes a covenant promise to Abram. The Lord changed Abram and Sarah name to Abraham and Sarah, Genesis 17. In chapter 18, the Lord assured Abraham that he would have a son by Sarah. Abraham was 100 years old when Isaac was born.

Starting in Genesis 17, the name "Abraham" is mentioned in some shape or form in the King James Bible 118 times. His name means "father of a multitude."

Note of Interests: The Book of Exodus has a total of 40 chapters. Even though Exodus has an 11th chapter, it only contains 10 verses. The Book of Exodus narrates how Moses led the Israelites out of Egypt, and later records the building of the Tabernacle based on God's instructions.

～～～～～～～～～～～

Chapter 4

LEVITICUS 11:29

**These also shall be unclean unto you among the
creeping things that creep upon the earth;
the weasel, and the mouse, and the
tortoise after his kind.**
Leviticus 11:29 KJV

~~~

The Book of Leviticus was written between 1440 – 1400 BC, and it is the 3rd book of the King James Bible. The Book of Leviticus contains laws relating to ceremonial observance conducted by the priests and Levites. The title "Leviticus" is derived from the "Tribe of Levi;" the Levites.

A Levite is a Jewish male who is a member of the Israelite Tribe of Levi; a descended from Levi who was the third son of Jacob and Leah. Levi's sons were Gershon, Kohath, and Merari. Levi was also the great-grandfather of Aaron and Moses. Aaron and Moses' father were named Amram, and his father was Kohath, the 2nd son of Levi.

The Levites were set aside by the Lord to be His priests and worship leaders at the Tabernacle, and later at the Temple of Jerusalem. According to Number 1, whenever the tabernacle was to be move, the Levites where to take it down and set it up. Anyone else who approaches it would be put to death.

Note of Interests: The Book of Leviticus is the first book studied by a Jewish child.

~~~~~~~~~~~~

Most of Leviticus consists of God's speeches to Moses, in which he is commanded to repeat to the Israelites, especially in chapters 1 – 7, and 11 – 27. The Israelites had been in captivity in Egypt for 400 years, and the many pagan Egyptian gods had distorted their concept of God. God instructed Moses, the Israelites and their priests how to make an offering in the Tabernacle, how to serve him and how to conduct themselves, morally. These instructions were given after they escaped Egypt and reached Mount Sinai, Exodus 19.

Note of Interests: The words, "The LORD spake to Moses" is mentioned on 38 occasions in the Book of Leviticus which consist of 27 chapters. It is mentioned at least once in every chapter, except Leviticus 2, 3, 20, and 26.

~~~~~~~~~~~~

Throughout the Book of Leviticus, the people were camped at the foot of Mount Sinai in the desert Peninsula of Sinai. According to Exodus 20, this is where the 10 commandments were given to Moses. Mount Sinai is also referred to as Mount Horeb, the Mountain of God where Moses saw the burning bush, Exodus 3. According to 1 Kings 19, the Prophet Elijah fled to Mount Sinai after slaying the prophets of Baal which belonged to Queen Jezebel.

Perfect Time to Mention: The book titled <u>Isaiah 26:3-4, "Perfect Peace XIII" 1st Kings 19:1-18</u> by Vanessa Rayner. It's the 13th book in a series called Isaiah 26:3-4, "Perfect Peace." This particular book speaks on Mount Sinai, Mount Horeb, Moses and the burning bush, the Prophet Elijah, the gods and prophets of Baal, Queen Jezebel, etc.

I believe you will enjoy reading it.

The 11th chapter of Leviticus consists of 47 verses. The entire chapter speaks on clean and unclean foods, spoken to Moses and Aaron by the Lord. The 11th chapter of Leviticus can be outlined as follows:

I. Leviticus 11:1 – 8, speaks on rules about eating meat.
II. Leviticus 11:9 – 12, speaks on rules about eating seafood.
III. Leviticus 11:13 – 19, mentions birds that must not be eaten.
IV. Leviticus 11:20 – 26, are the rules about eating insects.
V. Leviticus 11:26 – 28, speaks about more rules about animals.
VI. Leviticus 11:29 – 31, contains rules about crawling animals.
VII. Leviticus 11:32 – 47, are the rules about unclean animals.

The 29th verse of Leviticus mentions other unclean things, and it is written below.

<u>Leviticus 11:29 NIV</u>

"Of the animals that move along the ground, these are unclean for you: the weasel, the rat, and any kind of great lizard."

Note of Interests: Matthew 8:4, Luke 2:22, Luke 2:24, and Hebrews 8:5 are several verses in the New Testament that make references to "The Laws of Moses" found in the Book of Leviticus. For example: Luke 2:22 NLT reads, "Then it was time for the purification offering, as required by the Law of Moses after the birth of a child (Jesus); so, his parents (Joseph and Mary) took him to Jerusalem to present him to the Lord." *Hallelujah!*

~~~~~~~~~~~

Chapter 5

NUMBERS 11:29

And Moses said unto him, Enviest thou for my sake?
would God that all the Lord's people were prophets,
and that the Lord would put his spirit upon them!
Numbers 11:29 KJV

~~~

The Book of Numbers is a history of events that happened during the period of Israel wandering and camping in the wilderness for 40 years. The Book of Numbers obtained its name from the census that occurred twice among the tribes of Israel. The first census was taken in the 2nd month of the 2nd year after the Exodus, Numbers 1. The 2nd census was taken in the 40th year after the Exodus, Number 26.

The Books of Numbers primarily bridges the space and time between the Israelites receiving the Law in the books of Exodus and Leviticus to preparing them to enter the Promised Land. After the Israelites received the law at Mount Sinai, they began the journey and were ready to enter the land of Canaan, the Promised Land. When the Israelites went through various trials and tests, they became sinful. Their sinful ways resulted in them wandering in and through the wilderness 37 years.

The Book of Numbers concludes with the Israelites again at the edge of the land of Canaan. There they received instructions for the conquest of Canaan. After several battles, the conquered land was divided among them.

The Book of Numbers was written around 1450 – 1410 BC. The well-known individuals in this book include Moses, Aaron, Miriam Joshua, Caleb, Eleazar, Korah, Balak, and Balaam.

Apostle Paul called special attention to the Book of Numbers in 1 Corinthians 10:1 – 12, "Warnings from Israel's Idolatry History."

> **These things happened to them as examples and were written down as warnings for us, on whom the culmination of the ages has come.**
> 1 Corinthians 10:11 NIV

The Book of Numbers has 36 chapters, and a brief outline is listed below.

Chapters 1 thru 9:   The Israelites are preparing for their journey to enter the promised land. The first census of all the tribes is taken in chapter 1. The Levites are appointed to serve in the Tabernacle of the congregation. The offering of gifts from the tribes is mentioned in this section. The observance of the Passover at Sinai occurred in chapter 9 of Numbers.

Chapters 10 thru 12:   The Israelites travel from the wilderness in Sinai to Kadesh-Barnea to approach the promised land. The people of Israel complained about their food, so God gave them quail. The rebellion against Moses by Miriam and Aaron is recorded in Number 12.

Chapter 13 thru19:   The Israelites suffer severe punishment for being disobedience and unfaithful to God. Moses sends out 12 spies to explore the Promised Land. When the 12 spies return, only two had favorable news. Israel feared the inhabitants of the area and refused to enter the Promised Land. Therefore, God allowed them to roam in the wilderness for 40 years.

Chapter 20 thru 36:   Numbers 20 begins with Israel 40th years in the wilderness. They were basically back at the place where they were 38 years ago. They lodged at Kadesh which was near the borders of Canaan. The new generation of Israelites entered the land and destroyed the Canaanites and Amorites in battle. When King Balak heard what Israel had done to the Canaanites and Amorites, he summoned Balaam in order to curse the Israelites, but he couldn't curse what God had blessed, Numbers 22 – 24. According to Numbers 25, Balak used his prophet Balaam to learn how to entice the Israelites to worship Baal. When Israel began to worship Baal and indulge in sexual immorality with Moabite women, the Lord's anger burned against them and 24,000 people died. At the end of the Book of Numbers, Moses conducts the 2nd census. After Moses died, Joshua became the leader of Israel. God didn't allow Moses to enter the Promised Land, due to his disobedience. God commanded Moses to speak to the rock to obtain water for the people, but he strikes the rock with his staff, instead.

The 11th chapter of the Book of Numbers is divided into several sections.

    I.   The Israelites Complain vs. 1 – 3
    II. The Complaints about Food vs. 4 – 9
    III. Moses' Complaints to the Lord vs. 10 – 15
    IV. The Response of God, vs. 16 – 25
    V.   Eldad and Medad, vs. 26 – 30
    VI. Provision of Quail, vs. 31 – 35

The 29th verse of Number 11 reads as follows, But Moses replied, "Are you jealous for my sake? I wish that all the Lord's people were prophets and that the Lord would put his Spirit on them!" NIV

The biblical event surrounding this verse is as follows: Two men remained in the camp that didn't go to the tabernacle. One was named Eldad, and the other man was named Medad. The spirit of the Lord rested on them, and they prophesied in the camp. A young man ran and told Moses that they were prophesying in the camp. The young man asked Moses to stop them. Numbers 11:29 was the response Moses gave the young man. Then Moses returned to the camp along with the elders of Israel.

Chapter 6

DEUTERONOMY 11:29

And it shall come to pass, when the Lord they God hath brought thee in unto the land whither thou goest to possess it, that thou shalt put the blessing upon mount Gerizim, and the curse upon mount Ebal.
Deuteronomy 11:29 KJV

~~~

The Book of Deuteronomy is the 5th book of the Old Testament and considered the 5th and last "Book of the Law" written by Moses. The other four "Books of the Law" are Genesis, Exodus, Leviticus, and Numbers. The Books of the Law are also known by the following names, "Pentateuch," "The Law," "The Five Books of Moses," and "Torah."

The word "Deuteronomy" means "second law" but this is not a new law. It is the retelling of the law which was given to Moses at Mt. Sinai. It was done through 3 messages spoken by Moses. The people living during the messages in Deuteronomy were a new generation of Israelites who were very young or not born when the Law was initially given to Moses 40 years before.

The Old Testament and the New Testament refer to Moses as the author of the Books of the Law. Even though there are proofs that Moses wrote the book, someone else had to write the last chapter which mentions the death of Moses. Most Bible Scholars believed it was Joshua.

The teaching of "The Law" by Moses in Deuteronomy is quoted 90 times in 14 of the 27 books of the New Testament. Even Jesus when Satan tempted him in the Gospel of Luke, chapter 4, quoted from the Book of Deuteronomy; Deuteronomy 8:3, Deuteronomy 6:13 and Deuteronomy 6:16.

The Book of Deuteronomy covers approximately one month in the 40th year of the Israelites in the wilderness, Deuteronomy 1:3. The Book of Deuteronomy has been called the "Book of Remembrance." The biblical events of this book were written just before Moses death in 1406 BC around the time Israel was preparing to enter the land of Canaan for battle.

The Book of Deuteronomy contains farewell messages, also known as speeches and many times called sermons made by the leader, Moses, who was 120 years-old, now. In these three messages, Moses reminds the people of all the things God had done for Israel and the requirement to be the blessings God wanted to give his people, then he gave a prophecy to each of the 12 tribes. The Israelites were camped in the Plains of Moab, and these are the messages that Moses gave to them before entering Canaan, the Promised Land.

<u>Deuteronomy 11:29 NIV</u>

When the Lord your God has brought you into the land you are entering to possess you are to proclaim on Mount Gerizim the blessings, and on Mount Ebal the curses.

<u>Deuteronomy 11:29 NLT</u>

When the Lord your God brings you into the land and helps you take possession of it, you must pronounce the blessing at Mount Gerizim and the curse at Mount Ebal.

Historical Books of the Bible

There are 12 Historical Books in the King James Bible. The first 3 books of the 12 are Joshua, Judges, Ruth. They record the earliest history of the Jews. They cover the period when Israel was ruled by God from 1405 – 1043 BC; about 362 years.

The next 6 books of the Historical Books cover about 500 years. They are 1st Samuel, 2nd Samuel, 1st Kings, 2nd Kings, 1st Chronicles, and 2nd Chronicles.

First Chronicles along with Second Chronicles recount the history of Israel, Solomon, building of the temple, Israel split into two kingdoms, and the exile of Judah into Babylonian slavery around 586 BC.

The last 3 Historical Books of the 12 books are Ezra, Nehemiah, and Esther.

They described the return of a remnant to the land after 70 years of captivity from 605 to 536 BC. They are about their life in captivity, release from it, and the restoration of Jerusalem.

The books of Ezra and Nehemiah, along with Haggai, Zechariah, and Malachi are commonly called "post-exilic books." These books were written in Jerusalem after the return from the exile.

The books of Judges, 1st Kings, 1st Chronicles, and Nehemiah have an 11th chapter and 29th verse. However, the books of

Joshua, 1st Samuel, 2nd Samuel, 2nd Kings and 2nd Chronicles have an 11th chapter, but no 29th verse. The other Historical Books are Ruth with only 4 chapters, along with Ezra and Esther with 10 chapters.

Chapter 7

JUDGES 11:29

Then the Spirit of the Lord came upon Jephthah, and he passed over Gilead, and Manasseh, and passed over Mizpeh of Gilead, and from Mizpeh of Gilead he passed over unto the children of Ammon.
Judges 11:29 KJV

~~~

The Book of Judges is the 7th book of the King James Bible and has 21 chapters. The Book of Judges give the first 300 years of history of Israel starting from the death of Joshua to the time of Samuel, the last of the Judges. Judges bridge the period of time when the people of Israel had settled into their inheritance but before they were given a king.

The Book of Judges' title refers to the history of the deliverance and government of Israel by men who bore the title "Judge." The Book of Judges doesn't state who wrote the book. Some scholars believed that the prophets Nathan and Gad, who were associated with David's court helped in the writing of Judges, but many scholars believe it was the prophet Samuel, 1 Chronicles 29:29. Samuel was the last of the judges who God raised up during this era to rescue His people. In Bible days, the Judges didn't merely oversee legal issues, but was a military leader and over military services, as well.

The Book of Judges is viewed as a continuation to the Book of Joshua. The period of the Judges began after the death of Joshua around 1245 BC and continued until Saul was crowned king of Israel by the prophet Samuel approximately 1051 BC, 1 Samuel 10:24. The events in Judges stretches across the territorial regions of Israel. It reveals the adventures, affairs, and development that happened in and around the cities, towns, villages, and battlegrounds.

The Book of Judges reveals how Israel quickly forgot the acts of God that had established them in the land. The Sovereignty of God and the Israelites relationship to God had been uniquely set by the covenant at Mount Sinai, Exodus 19 – 24, which was later restated by Moses on the plains of Moab in Deuteronomy 29, and then by Joshua at Shechem, Joshua 24. They lost sight of their unique identity as God's people. Israel attached themselves to Canaanites and their morals, gods, and religious beliefs and practices. They stopped fighting the Lord's battles against the enemies, turned to the gods of Canaan to secure their blessings for family, livestock, and crops. They abandoned God's law which governs their worship and daily living. Therefore, God would use foreign oppressors to chasten his people by delivering them into the hand of their enemies. Therefore, implementing the covenant curses mentioned in Leviticus 26:14 – 45 and Deuteronomy 28:15 – 68.

The people of Israel would repent and plead with God for mercy. God would then raise up a judge to deliver them from their oppressors. The Israelites would prosper for a while, but soon they would fall again into this sinful and unfaithful cycle.

The Book of Judges can be outlined in several ways. A simple outline is listed below.

The Condition of Israel Under the Judges	-	Joshua 1:1 to 3:6
The Judges of Israel	-	Joshua 3:7 to 16:31
The Sinfulness of Israel	-	Joshua 17:1 to 21:25

Judges 11:29 verse is found in the section titled <u>The Judges of Israel</u>. The verse reads as follows, "At the time the Spirit of the Lord came upon Jephthah, and he went throughout the land of Gilead and Manasseh, including Mizpah in Gilead, and from there he led an army against the Ammonites." NLT

The biblical event that surrounds this verse is captivating. Jephthah the Gileadite was a mighty and gifted warrior. He was the product of his father, Gilead, sexual affair with a prostitute. His half-brothers rejected him, and he fled to Israel and lived on the outskirts.

When the Ammonites threatened the Gileadites with war, the elders overcame their dislike for Jephthah. They humbled themselves, begged him to defend them, and agreed that he would become their leader, Judges 11:4 – 11.

Even though Jephthah was a rugged man, he was a man of faith. According to Judges 11:9, he acknowledged that if he defeated the Ammonites, it would be because the Lord gave him the victory.

Jephthah tried to settle the Ammonites' grievance with Israel peacefully. He appealed to the king of Ammon with 3 arguments which are listed below.

1st Argument:	The Ammonites had no right to Israel's territory east of the Jordan River.
2nd Argument:	He emphasized the fact that God had given Israel this land.
3rd Argument:	If Ammon had a legitimate claim to this land, why didn't they seize it 300 years ago?

When the Ammonite king disregarded Jephthah's messages, he called on the Lord, Judges 11:27 – 28. According to Judges 11:29, the Spirit of the Lord then clothed Jephthah, and he traveled through the area of Gilead and Manasseh. He went through the city of Mizpah on his way to the land of the Ammonites. The Lord gave Jephthah and his army victory in the battle, and he destroyed 20 cities in Ammon. The Ammonites stronghold was broken, so they ceased oppressing Israel, Judge 11:33.

Chapter 8

1 KINGS 11:29

**And it came to pass at that time when Jeroboam
went out of Jerusalem, that the prophet Ahijah
the Shilonite found him in the way;
and he had clad himself with a new garment;
and they two were alone in the field:**
1 Kings 11:29 KJV

~~~

King David, a mighty warrior, had conquered Israel's
enemies, and they had peace and prosperity in the land. It
was the promised land of God's chosen people, Israel. First
Kings is viewed as the continuation to 1st and 2nd Samuel.
It was written between 560 and 540 BC. Jewish tradition
believes Jeremiah, the prophet is the author of 1st Kings.
Bible scholars are divided on this issue, and others think
a group of anonymous authors called the Deuteronomist
wrote 1st King.

First King has 22 chapters; recorded in these chapters are 4
major events, King David's death, King Solomon's reign, the
division of the kingdom, and Elijah's ministry. The Book of
1st Kings covers approximately 120-years; the beginning of
King Solomon's reign in 971 BC, through King Ahaziah's
reign ending in 851 BC.

According to 1ˢᵗ Kings 4, King Solomon received extraordinary wisdom and great insight from God. He built a magnificent temple, increased trade, and became the wealthiest man of his time. According to 1ˢᵗ Kings 11, Solomon married many foreign wives, who led him away from the worship of God. Idolatry has disastrous consequences and causes ruin to both individuals and nations.

First Kings also records the fall of King Solomon due to his involvement with the false gods and pagan customs of his foreign wives. First Kings describes the reign of King David's son, Solomon. He was the last king of Israel before they split into two kingdoms, after his death. In 931 BC the 12 tribes of Israel became a divided kingdom, which created 2 nations with 2 set of kings. The Northern Kingdom was called Israel with 10 tribes, and the Southern Kingdom was called the Kingdom of Judah with 2 tribes, Benjamin and Judah.

According to 1ˢᵗ Kings 12, Israel rebels against Rehoboam. The division of Israel came about because King Solomon had burdened the people with heavy taxes. After his death, the people wanted his son, Rehoboam to lighten the harsh labor and remove the heavy taxes. King Rehoboam refused and decided to make things even harder for the people. His actions caused 10 tribes of the 12 tribes of Israel to break away and form their kingdom under the leadership of Jeroboam who became their 1ˢᵗ king. The tribes of Benjamin and Judah remained with Solomon's son, King Rehoboam.

Beginning in 1ˢᵗ Kings 17, Elijah the prophet sternly warned Israel of God's wrath over their disobedience. The kings and the people did not want to repent and acknowledge their sins. A few kings were righteous and tried to lead the people back to God.

Note of Interests: Out of all the northern and southern kings mentioned in 1ˢᵗ Kings only Asa and Jehoshaphat did what is "right in the eyes of the Lord," 1 Kings 15:9 – 16 and 1 Kings 22:41 – 45.

~~~~~~~~~~~

The Book of 1ˢᵗ Kings has 22 chapters. A brief outline of 1ˢᵗ Kings is listed below.

1 Kings 1 – 2	David's death, Solomon's ascent as king
1 Kings 3 – 4	Solomon's wisdom and government
1 Kings 5 – 8	Building the Temple and Palace
1 Kings 9 – 12	Solomon's Wives and His Downfall
1 Kings 13	Northern Tribes Revolt
1 Kings 14 – 16	Deeds of Kings of Israel and Judah
1 Kings 17 – 21	Ministry of Elijah
1 Kings 22	Kings of Israel and Judah, Ahab's Death

The biblical event surrounding 1 Kings 11:29 is embedded in Solomon's wives and his downfall. The NIV verse reads as follows, "About that time Jeroboam was going out of Jerusalem, and Ahijah the prophet of Shiloh met him on the way, wearing a new cloak. The two of them were alone out in the country."

The remainder of this chapter tells us that Ahijah took hold of the cloak Jeroboam was wearing and tore it into 12 pieces. The prophet told Jeroboam that 10 pieces were for him. The Lord, the God of Israel, was going to rip the kingdom out of Solomon's hand and give him 10 tribes out of the 12.

The prophet then told Jeroboam the Lord was doing this because Israel has forsaken him. They were worshipping Ashtoreth the goddess of the Sidonians, Chemosh the god of the Moabites, and Molek, god of the Ammonites.

Solomon tried to kill Jeroboam, but he fled to Egypt and lived there until Solomon death. Rehoboam, Solomon's son, succeeded him, chapter 11. In 1 Kings 12, Israel rebels against Rehoboam. The kingdom was divided, and Jeroboam became their king.

Note of Interests: 2nd Kings the 11th chapter only has 21 verses. It's an interesting chapter. The 1st verse reads, "And when Athaliah the mother of Ahaziah saw that her son was dead, she arose and destroyed all the seed royal." Also, in the original Hebrew Bible, the books of 1st and 2nd Kings were originally one book.

Chapter 9

1 CHRONICLES 11:29

Sibbecai the Hushathite, Ilai the Ahohite,
1 Chronicles 11:29 KJV

~~~

The Book of 1st Chronicles is believed by most scholars to be written by Ezra, probably written shortly, after Israel returned from the Babylonian Exile between 450 and 425 BC. It was written to help those returning to Israel understand how to worship God, and it speaks on the priestly responsibilities.

Note of Interests: The Books of 1st and 2nd Chronicles cover mostly the same information as 1st and 2nd Samuel and 1st and 2nd Kings. The Book of 1st and 2nd Chronicles were one book in the Hebrew Bible. The Book of 1st and 2nd Samuel and 1st and 2nd Kings were also one book until it was translated into Greek, the Septuagint.

~~~~~~~~~~~

The majority of 1 Chronicles' history surrounds the Southern Kingdom which consisted of two tribes; Judah, and Benjamin. The tribes of Judah and Benjamin along with the Levi were the most faithful to God compared to the Northern Kingdom.

Let's name the 10 tribes of the Northern Kingdom: *smile*

1. _____
2. _____
3. _____
4. _____
5. _____
6. _____
7. _____
8. _____
9. _____
10. _____

Answer in the back of the book

The name "Chronicles" means "Acts and Events of the Days." The first 9 chapters of 1 Chronicles list genealogies in the line of Israel. Chapter 10 speaks of Saul and his son's death in the battle with the Philistines. David's reign and deeds are recorded in 1 Chronicles, chapters 11 thru 29.

The Book of 1st Chronicles, the 11th chapter begins with David crowned king over Israel, vs. 1 – 3. The next section of 1 Chronicles 11 is describing how David conquers Jerusalem with the Israelites, vs. 4 – 9. David's mighty warriors are identified and listed in vs. 10 – 47. 1 Chronicles 11:29, is where Sibbekai the Hushathite, and Ilai the Ahohite's names are recorded as one of David's mighty warrior.

Sibbecai name is also spelled "Sibbekai" in other Bible translations. His name is mentioned once more in the King James Bible, 1 Chronicles 27:11. There he is described as the 8th captain for the 8th month with 24,000 men in his division.

The NIV (New International Version) mentions in 2 Samuel 21:18 and 1 Chronicles 20:4, that Sibbekai the Hushathite killed Saph, the father of giants, one of the descendants of Rapha. Sibbekai name is also mentioned in 2 Samuel 23:27, as a mighty warrior of David. Ilai the Ahohite is only mentioned in 1 Chronicles 11, KJV.

Note of Interests: The Book of 2nd Chronicles has 36 chapter, but its 11th chapter only has 23 verses. This chapter is concerning Shemaiah the prophet.

He warns Rehoboam in verses 1 thru 5. In verses 6 thru 12, Rehoboam fortifies the cities in Judah. In the next section, verses 13-17, the priests and the Levites support Rehoboam. In the last section, Rehoboam's family is mentioned, verses 18 thru 23. He had 18 wives and 60 concubines. He fathered 28 sons and 60 daughters. The Book of Ezra only has 10 chapters.

~~~~~~~~~~~

Take a break and read the 11th chapter of 2 Chronicles? *smile*

Chapter 10

NEHEMIAH 11:29

And at Enrimmon, and at Zareah, and at Jarmuth,
Nehemiah 11:29 KJV

~~~

The Book of Nehemiah is the last Historical Book of the Old Testament. It was initially part of the Book of Ezra until it was separated in the 3rd century AD by the Christian scholar Origen. Many scholars believe that Ezra wrote both books, and others credit Ezra as the author of the book, using Nehemiah's memoirs in parts of it. The Book of Ezra consists of 10 chapters, and the Book of Nehemiah has 13 chapters. The Book of Nehemiah describes the biblical events that occurred while the people were rebuilding Jerusalem's wall in 444 BC, during the Second Temple period.

Note of Interests: Solomon built the First Temple in 10 BC. The Babylonians destroyed it around 586 BC. The Second Temple was reconstructed around 516 BC by King Herod on the site of the First Temple and destroyed in 70 AD, by the Romans. During the Second Temple period the Pharisees, Sadducees, Essenes, and Zealots were formed.

~~~~~~~~~~~

Nehemiah has 13 chapters, and can be outlined as follows:

Nehemiah 1 – 2

Nehemiah journey to Jerusalem to rebuild the wall of Jerusalem.

Nehemiah 3

The names of those who repaired the gates.

Nehemiah 4:1 – Nehemiah 7:4

The opposition led by Sanballat, Tobiah, and Geshem against the wall.

Nehemiah 7

The names of the exiles who returned with Zerubbabel.

Nehemiah 8

Ezra reads the Book of the Law of Moses.

Nehemiah 9:1 – Nehemiah 10:39

The people of Israel repent.

Nehemiah 11:1 – Nehemiah 12:26

The name of the people who moved into Jerusalem.

Nehemiah 12:27 – Nehemiah 12:47

The dedication of the wall of Jerusalem.

Nehemiah 13

Nehemiah's final reforms.

Nehemiah was a remarkable individual in the Book of Nehemiah. He was a Jewish cupbearer at the Persian court in Judea under Artaxerxes I of Persia around 444 BC, Nehemiah 1:11. The name Nehemiah means "comforter."

Nehemiah heard from his brother Hanani that the walls in Jerusalem were broken down and fire had destroyed its gates. Nehemiah mourned, fasted and prayed before God of heaven, Nehemiah 1:4. Nehemiah afterward asked the king for permission to return to the city of Judah, so he could rebuild it. Later that year, Nehemiah traveled to Israel, leading the 3rd of the three returns by the Jewish people following their 70 years of exile in Babylon with an armed escort, supplies, and letters from the king, Nehemiah 2.

Note of Interests: The previous chapters in Ezra describes the earlier two returns. Nehemiah was a layman, not a priest like Ezra, nor a prophet like Malachi.

~~~~~~~~~~~~

Nehemiah along with the people met opposition immediately from Sanballat the Horonite, Tobiah, the Arabs, the Ammonite, and the people of Ashdod, who feared a fortified Jerusalem. In an inspiring speech to the Jews, Nehemiah convinced them to continue to rebuild the wall, Nehemiah 4-6.

The people worked hard in rebuilding the wall of Jerusalem. They were armed with weapons, in case of an attack. In 52 days, the wall was finished. Ezra, the priest, and the scribes read the Law of Moses to the people. The people repented, confessed their sins and worshiped God. Nehemiah and Ezra re-established civil and religious practices in Jerusalem, preparing the city for the Jews return.

The 11th chapter of Nehemiah can be outlined as follows:

I.   The People Living in Jerusalem, vs. 1-25
II. The People Living on the Outskirts of Jerusalem, vs. 26-36

The NLT (New Living Translation) of Nehemiah 11:29 and 30 are written below. The 30th verse has been added to help make the 29th verse understandable. These verses are stating where some of the people lived and dwelled on the outskirts of Jerusalem when they returned.

Nehemiah 11:29-30 NLT

29. They also lived in En-rimmon, Zorah, Jarmuth, 30. Zanoah, and Adullam with their surrounding villages. They also lived in Lachish with its nearby fields and Azekah with its surrounding villages. So, the people of Judah were living all the way from Beersheba in the south to the valley of Hinnom.

Note of Interests: The next book in the Bible that has an 11th chapter with a 29th verse is Proverbs. The books that are in between Nehemiah and Proverbs are Esther, Job, and Psalms. Esther has 10 chapters, Job has 42 chapters, but the 11th chapter only has 20 verses, and Psalms has 150 chapters, but the 11th chapter only has 7 verses.

~~~~~~~~~~~~

The 5 Poetic Books of the Bible

Job has 42 chapters, but the 11th chapter consists of 20 verses. It is a book that confronts the problem of human sufferings and the sovereignty of God.

Psalms have 150 chapters, but the 11th chapter has 7 verses. This book is filled with beautiful poetry describing human problems, and prayers.

Proverbs has 31 chapters. It's packed with God's wisdom for living life. Proverbs is the only Poetic Book with an 11th chapter and a 29th verse.

Ecclesiastes has 12 chapters, but the 11th chapter has 10 verses. It's a book that approaches the pursuit of meaning in life.

Song of Songs sometimes called "Song of Solomon" has 8 chapters. It portraits love and affection within marriage.

Chapter 11

PROVERBS 11:29

**He that troubleth his own house shall inherit the wind:
and the fool shall be servant to the wise of heart.**
Proverbs 11:29 KJV

~~~

King Solomon, the son of King David, is acknowledged as one of the writers of Proverbs. The other writers include a group of men called "The Wise," Agur, and King Lemuel. The word "Proverb" comes from a Hebrew word meaning "to be like" or "to represent." The Book of Proverbs urges readers to make decisions based on wisdom, justice, and righteousness, Proverbs 1:3.

The Book of Proverbs was written around 971 – 931 BC. Although, the material in the Book of Proverbs was not compiled until centuries later, probably during the time of King Hezekiah 728 – 686 BC, based on Proverbs 25:1.

**"These also are proverbs of Solomon which the
men of Hezekiah king of Judah copied."**
Proverbs 25:1 KJV

When Solomon became the new king of Israel, God appeared to him in a dream at Gibeon and said, "Ask for whatever you wish me to give you." 1 Kings 3:5. Solomon could have asked for long life, wealth unspeakable, the death of all his enemies, but instead, he asked God for wisdom to govern Israel, 1 Kings 3:9. God was pleased with his request and granted it to him. Solomon ruled with wisdom and justice and all Israel prosperous, 1 Kings 4:20 – 25.

According to 1 Kings 4:30, Solomon's wisdom surpassed the wisdom of all the sons of the east and all the wisdom of Egypt. He spoke 3,000 proverbs about trees, animals, birds, creeping things, fish, mankind, work, money, marriage, friendship, family life, perseverance, and pleasing God.

The Book of Proverbs speaks on various types of people. It mentions behaviors that should be avoided, and behaviors that should be imitated. Although Proverbs was written in Israel thousands of years ago, its wisdom is still relevant, today. A brief outline of the Book of Proverbs is as follows:

Proverbs 1 – 9   Wisdom for Young People
Proverbs 10 – 24   Wisdom on Various Topics
Proverbs 25 – 29   Wisdom to Leaders
Proverbs 30   Wisdom from Agur
Proverbs 31   Wisdom from King Lemuel and
                        the Ideal Wife

Proverbs 11:29 is embedded in "Wisdom on Various Topics." It reads:
Whoever brings ruin on their family will inherit only wind, and the fool will be a servant to the wise. NIV

Verse 29 is implying, a person who causes or bring trouble to his family will be unable to keep and enjoy what he has, this statement is being compared to a man who is unable to hold the wind. The next section of this verse is saying that a foolish person will eventually be the servant to a wise person.

Note of Interests: The New Testament makes references to the Book of Proverbs approximately 60 times, and several examples are given below.

James 4:6 Be he giveth more grace. Wherefore he saith, God resisteth the proud, but giveth grace unto the humble. <u>Proverbs 3:34</u> Surely, he scorneth the scorners: but he giveth grace unto the lowly.

1 Peter 4:8 And above all things have fervent charity among yourselves: for charity shall cover the multitude of sins. <u>Proverbs 10:12</u> Hatred stirreth up strife: but love covereth all sins.

2 Peter 2:22 Of them the proverbs are true: "A dog returns to its vomit," and, "A sow that is washed returns to her wallowing in the mud." <u>Proverbs 26:11</u> As a dog returns to its vomit, so fools repeat their follow.

Romans 2:6 Who will render to every man according to his deeds. <u>Proverbs 24:12</u> If thou sayest, Behold, we knew it not; doth not he that pondereth the heart consider it? And he that keepeth thy soul, doth not he knows it? And shall not he render to every man according to his works?

Hebrews 12:5,6   And ye have forgotten the exhortation which speaketh unto you as unto children, my son, despise not thou the chastening of the Lord, nor faint when thou art rebuked of him: For whom the Lord loveth he chasteneth, and scourgeth every son whom he receiveth. <u>Proverbs 3:11,12</u>   My son, despise not chastening of the Lord; neither be weary of his correction: For whom the Lord loveth he correcteth; even as a father the son in whom he delighteth.

~~~~~~~~~~~~

The 5 Major Prophets' Books

The titles "Major Prophets" and "Minor Prophets" are used to distinguish the longer books of prophecy in the Old Testament from the shorter books. These books are centered on a particular prophet, and generally, it's the prophet who wrote the book.

The 5 Major Prophets' Books are Isaiah with 66 chapters, Jeremiah with 52 chapters, Lamentations with 5 chapters, Ezekiel with 48 chapters and Daniel with 12 chapters. The Book of Lamentations is a collection of poetic laments about the destruction of Jerusalem, and most scholars believe Jeremiah wrote it.

Note of Interests: The Twelve Minor Prophets' Books were once grouped as a single book in the Hebrew Bible but was separated into 12 individual books in the Christian, Old Testament Bible. The Hebrew Bible or Hebrew Scriptures is the phrase used by biblical scholars to refers to the Tanakh; the orthodoxy collection of Jewish texts which consists of 24 books. The books of the Tanakh were passed on by each generation, by an oral tradition called the Oral Torah.

~~~~~~~~~~~~

Chapter 12

DANIEL 11:29

At the time appointed he shall return,
and come toward the south;
but it shall not be as the former, or as the latter.
Daniel 11:29 KJV

~~~

Out of the five Major Prophets' books, the Book of Daniel is the only one with an 11th chapter and 29th verse. The verse reads as follows:

NIV: **At the appointed time he will invade the South again, but this time the outcome will be different from what it was before.**

NLT: **Then at the appointed time he will once again invade the south, but this time the result will be different.**

The Book of Daniel surrounds biblical events in Daniel's life. His name means "God Is My Judge." The Book of Daniel can be divided into 2 parts; chapters 1 thru 6, records the courageous acts and deeds of young Daniel and his three friends; Shadrach, Meshack, and Abednego. Then chapters 7 thru 12, deals with 4 apocalyptic visions of the future seen by Daniel.

Daniel was carried off to Babylon in 605 BC by King Nebuchadnezzar, the Assyrian, after the destruction of Jerusalem around the age of 15. Once Daniel arrived in Babylon, his named was changed to Belteshazzar, Daniel 1:7. The name means "Bel protects his life." Bel is one of the many gods of Babylon's god Babel.

Shortly after Daniel arrived in Babylon, Nebuchadnezzar has a troubling dream that his magicians and diviners couldn't interpret, Daniel 2. The king wouldn't even tell them what he dreamt. According to Daniel 2:10 – 12, the magicians said to the king, "No one can interpret your dream, except the gods, and they do not live among humans." The king was ready to have all of his magicians and diviners killed until Daniel prayed to the God of heaven to help him understand this secret, Daniel 2:12 – 23.

It wasn't long afterward that Daniel became one of only 3 chief administrators throughout the kingdom, Daniel 6:1. Also in Daniel 6 the other administrators plotted against him, and he was thrown into the lions' den, but God shut the lions' mouth. Daniel was probably in his 80's when he was thrown into the lions' den.

Daniel was the administrator under 4 different kings, while he was in exile in Babylon. Daniel was still living in Babylon when the Medes and Persians overthrew Assyria. Daniel lived there throughout the Jew's 70 years of captivity, Daniel 1:21, Daniel 9:2. The kings he served are listed follows:

1. Nebuchadnezzar, after Daniel interprets his dream, Daniel 2:48.
2. Belshazzar, after Daniel reads the handwriting on the wall, Daniel 5:29.
3. Darius the Mede, because of Daniel's "extraordinary spirit," Daniel 6:1 – 3.
4. Cyrus the Persian, for reasons unknown.

The Book of Daniel's chapters can be outlined as follows:

Chapter 1	Daniel's Captivity
Chapter 2	Nebuchadnezzar's Dream
Chapter 3	The Fiery Furnace
Chapter 4	Nebuchadnezzar's Vision
Chapter 5	Belshazzar's Feast
Chapter 6	Daniel in the Lion Den
Chapter 7	Daniel's Vision of the 4 Beasts
Chapter 8	Daniel's Vision of the Ram, Goat & Little Horn
Chapter 9	Daniel's Prophecy of 70 Weeks
Chapter 10, 11, 12	Daniel's Final Vision

The 11th chapter of Daniel can be divided into 4 sections.

I. Warring Kings of the North and South, Egypt, and Syria, vs. 1 – 4
II. Kings of the North and South Warring, Again, Egypt, and Syria, vs. 5 – 28
III. The Northern King's Blasphemies, vs. 29 – 39
IV. The Northern King's Conquests, vs. 40 – 45

The 29th verse of Daniel 11, is part of Daniel's final vision along with chapters 10, and 12. A series of wars between the unnamed "King of the North" and "King of the South" is being discussed. These wars will lead to the end-time. At the end-time, Israel will be justified, and the dead raised to shame or glory.

Chapter 10 is the introduction of Daniel's vision concerning what will happen to Israel in the future. Chapter 11, the angel Michael is telling Daniel, that there will be 3 more Persia kings, and the last king will make war with the kingdom of Greece. After this king will come a stronger and powerful king whose kingdom will be broken up and scattered in all directions, Daniel 11:1 – 5.

There will be wars and marriages among the kings of the South and North, but the king of the North will violate the sacredness of the Temple. This action will cause the abomination that causes desolation, Daniel 11:31. The king of the North will be defeated between the seas at the glorious holy mountain, Daniel 11:45.

Chapter 12 is where Daniel's vision ends. The Jews who names are found in the book of life will be saved, and the dead will awaken to everlasting shame or glory, Daniel 12:2.

Note of Interests: The Minor Prophets' Books are not called "minor" because they are irrelevant but because of the size. The Minor Prophets' Books are Hosea (14), Joel (3), Amos (9), Obadiah (1), Jonah (4), Micah (7), Nahum (3), Habakkuk (3), Zephaniah (3), Haggai (2), Zechariah (14) and Malachi (4). The books of Hosea and Zechariah has an 11th chapter, but no 29th verse. All these books warn of impending judgment because of sinfulness, described the sin, tells the coming judgment, makes a call for repentance, and gives a promise of future deliverance.

~~~~~~~~~~~~

The 4 Gospels

The Gospel According to Matthew is the 1st book in the New Testament. Matthew was one of the 12 Apostles of Jesus. The Book of Matthew is a narrative about Jesus' ministry in Galilee beginning with his genealogy.

The Gospel According to Mark is the 2nd book in the New Testament written by John Mark. He wasn't one of the Apostles of Jesus but a companion of Paul on some of his missionary journeys. Mark begins his account of Jesus by describing his adult life. It is traditionally believed that the Gospel of Mark is the oldest of the four Gospels.

The Gospel According to Luke is the 3rd book in the New Testament. Luke was a Greek physician and a traveling companion of Paul. Luke also wrote the Acts of the Apostles, and he is believed to be the only gentile author in the Bible.

The Gospel According to John is the 4th book in the New Testament. It is one of the four Canonical Gospels of the New Testament, but not considered among the Synoptic Gospels. The Synoptic Gospels are Matthew, Mark, and Luke. They include many of the same biblical events, in similar sequences and description. John's Gospel omits a vast number of events found in the Synoptic Gospels and includes mostly information that is not found in the other 3 Gospels.

Note of Interests: The Gospels are traditionally believed to be written as follows: Mark to be the 1ˢᵗ Gospel written around 60 AD. Matthew and Luke were written between 60 – 70 AD. John the last gospel was written between 90 – 100 AD.

Chapter 13

MATTHEW 11:29

Take my yoke upon you, and learn of me;
for I am meek and lowly in heart: and
ye shall find rest unto your souls.
Matthew 11:29 KJV

~~~

The Gospel According to Matthew is the 1st book in the New Testament. It is also called by the following titles, "Gospel of Matthew," "Book of Matthew," and "Matthew." Most scholars believe the Gospel of Matthew was composed between 60 and 70 AD. The Gospel of Matthew is one of the 3 Synoptic Gospels, and it has 28 chapters.

Matthew was a Jewish tax collector for the Romans before he became one of the 12 Apostles of Jesus. His name means "a gift of the Lord." Matthew a 1st century Galilean, the son of Alpheus was well educated, and he could read and write Aramaic and Greek. By Matthew being a tax collector, his fellow Jews despised and hated him for what was viewed as working with and for the Roman Empire.

According to Matthew 9:9, as Jesus was walking along, he saw a man named Matthew sitting at his tax collector's booth. Jesus said to him, "follow me and be my disciple." Matthew got up and followed him.

Note of Interests: Matthew is called by his other name, "Levi" in the Gospel of Mark and Luke.

~~~~~~~~~~~~

The Book of Matthew is a narrative about Jesus' ministry in Galilee beginning with his genealogy. Matthew's gospel goes back to Jesus' origins, showing him as the Son of God from his birth, the fulfillment of Old Testament messianic prophecies.

Matthew's describes how Jesus the Messiah was rejected by his own people of Israel, and the disciples were then sent to the whole world to preach the gospel.

The Gospel of Matthew can be outlined as follows:

I.   The Birth and Early Years of Jesus, Chapters 1 – 2
II.   The Beginnings of Jesus' Ministry, Chapter 3 – 4
III.   Jesus' Ministry in Galilee, Chapter 4 – 14
IV.   Jesus Withdrawals from Galilee, Chapter 14 – 17
V.   Jesus Last Ministry in Galilee, Chapter 17 – 18
VI.   Jesus Ministry in Judea and Perea, Chapter 19 – 20
VII.   Passion Week, Chapter 21 – 27
VIII. The Resurrection, Chapter 28

The 11th chapter of the Book of Matthew begins with John the Baptist in prison. He sent his messengers to Jesus with a question, vs. 1 – 19. The question was, "Are you the Messiah we have been expecting, or should we keep looking for someone else?" Matthew 11:3. Jesus replied, "Go back and tell John what you have heard and seen. The blind receive sight, the lame walk, lepers are cured, the deaf can hear, the dead are raised from the dead, and the "Good News" is being proclaimed to the poor. Great blessings belong to those who don't have a problem accepting me," Matthew 11:4 – 8.

Verses 20 – 24, in this chapter, is regarding Jesus speaking warnings to the people in the cities of Chorazin, Bethsaida, and Capernaum. The people refused to repent after seeing Jesus perform many miracles.

Note of Interests: The city of Chorazin was located in Galilee, 2½ miles from Capernaum on a hill above the northern coast of the Sea of Galilee. Bethsaida was a fishing village near the Sea of Galilee, 2 miles east of Capernaum. It was the hometown of Peter, Andrew, and Philip. Two of Jesus well-known miracles occurred near Bethsaida. A blind man was healed, and 5,000 men were fed, Mark 8 and Luke 9. Capernaum was a fishing village, located on the north-western coast of the Sea of Galilee, the city where Jesus lived. It's the area where Jesus chose several of His apostles; Peter, Andrew, John and James, Mark 1. In Capernaum, Jesus healed a man possessed by evil spirits, healed Peter's sick mother-in-law, and healed the centurion's servant. Chorazin, Bethsaida, and Capernaum are excavation sites, now.

~~~~~~~~~~~~

In the last section of chapter 11, verses 25 thru 30, Jesus is offering to give rest to his people that are weary and burdened. Jesus is trying to give them rest from the heavy burdens laid on them by the Pharisees. The people are trying to earn their way in heaven through self-righteousness and strict laws given by the Pharisees.

Matthew 23:4, Jesus rebukes the Pharisees for laying strict heavy burdens on the shoulders of the people to obey, which they don't follow themselves. According to biblical scholars, the Pharisees added over 600 rules regarding what is recognized as working on the Sabbath. They also added additional rules to the other "Laws of Moses."

Jesus tells the people that he is gentle and humble, his yoke is easy, the burden is light, and they will find rest for their souls. The 29th verse is part of this section.

Matthew 11:28 – 29 NLT

28. Then Jesus said, "Come to me, all of you who are weary and carry heavy burdens, and I will give you rest. 29. Take my yoke upon you. Let me teach you, because I am humble and gentle at heart, and you will find rest for your souls.

Chapter 14

MARK 11:29

And Jesus answered and said unto them, I will also ask of you one question, and answer me, and I will tell you by what authority I do these things.
Mark 11:29 KJV

~~~

The Gospel of Mark is the shortest book in the Gospel Synoptics; it contains 16 chapters. Mark's Gospel was written after Jesus' death with the help of Peter's eyewitness accounts. Mark became close to Peter as he ministered throughout Asia Minor and Rome. Mark acted as a scribe for Peter and recorded his teaching and preaching in the Gospel of Mark. By the time Peter wrote his first epistle, Mark had become like a son to him, 1 Peter 5:13.

She who is in Babylon, chosen together with you, sends you her greetings, and so does my son Mark.
1 Peter 5:13 KJV

Mark is also known as John Mark. He was the son of Mary, a religious woman living in Jerusalem who home is where the Apostles and 1st Christians assembled. Mark was also the cousin of Barnabas, Colossians 4:10. Mark also accompanied Paul and Barnabas on their missionary journeys, Acts 15.

Mark's Gospel is unique because its directed to the Gentile believers and emphasizes Jesus' actions more than His teaching. Many scholars believe that Mark wrote to bring the message of Jesus Christ to the Roman listeners and assemblies.

The Gospel of Mark reveals Jesus Christ as the Servant of the Lord, Savior of the World, and Son of God. It records Jesus' ministry from his baptism by John the Baptist to his death, burial, resurrection, and the discovery of the empty tomb. It gives detail of how Jesus, called his first 4 disciples, healed the sick, taught the multitudes, ministered to individual needs, and confronted the religious leaders.

Chapter 11 begins with Jesus and his disciples approaching Jerusalem. Jesus sent two of his disciples to the nearby village to find and bring him a colt that had never been ridden. When the disciples arrived with the colt, Jesus rode on it entering Jerusalem as the Messiah. The people spread branches on the road and shout "Hosanna!"

The 11th chapter of Mark could be outlined as follows:

    I.   Jesus' Triumph Entrance into Jerusalem, vs. 1 – 11
    II. Jesus Curses the Fig Tree, vs. 12 – 14
    III. Jesus Cleanses Temple of Money Changers, vs. 15 – 19
    IV. The Fig Tree Withered, vs. 20 – 24
    V. Forgiveness and Prayer, vs. 25 – 26
    VI. Jesus' Authority is Questioned, vs. 27 – 33

Jesus' Authority is Questioned, verses 27 - 33 is where the 29th verse of Mark 11 is embedded. This verse is the answer Jesus gave to the question by the rulers.

Mark 11:29 NLT

"I'll tell you by what authority I do these things if you answer one question," Jesus replied.

In brief, Jesus had just cleared the Temple courts of the merchants who were buying and selling there. He overturned the tables of the money changers. He turned over benches of those selling doves, and he refused to allow people to carry anything through the Temple courts.

Jesus began to teach the people. He mentioned, "It is written in the Scripture, My Temple will be called a house of prayer for all nations." Then Jesus told the people they had turned the Temple it into a "den of thieves." The crowd of people was astonished at Jesus' teaching.

When the chief priests, scribes, and elders heard what Jesus had done, they question him. They asked Jesus, "By what authority are you doing these things, and who gave you the authority to do this?"

According to Mark 11:29, 30, Jesus replied, "I will ask you one question. Answer me, and I will tell you by what authority I am doing these things. John's baptism was it from heaven, or of human origin? Tell me!

According to Mark 11:31, 32, the chief priests, scribes, and elders discussed it among themselves. They knew if they said it was from heaven, then Jesus would ask them why didn't they believe John the Baptist? And they were afraid to say that John acted on his own authority because the people believed that John was a prophet. So, the religious leaders decided to say, "We don't know," vs. 33. Then Jesus said, "Neither will I tell you by what authority I am doing these things."

John the Baptist was the forerunner of Jesus Christ, the Messiah. His mission was to prepare the way and announce his coming. John bare witnessed and proclaimed to all that Jesus was the Messiah, but the chief priests, scribes, and elders refused to believe. So, it really would have been of no avail for Jesus to declare his authority among them.

Chapter 15

LUKE 11:29

And when the people were gathered thick together,
he began to say, This is an evil generation:
they seek a sign; and there shall no sign be
given it, but the sign of Jonas the prophet.
Luke 11:29 KJV

~~~

Apostle Luke wrote the 3ʳᵈ Gospel, which is called the "Gospel of Luke" or simply "Luke." He wrote the Acts of the Apostles (Acts) which is viewed as a continuation of the Gospel of Luke, and they are both addressed to the same individual, Theophilus.

Having carefully investigated everything from the
beginning, I also have decided to write an accurate
account for you, most honorable Theophilus.
Luke 1:3 NLT

In my first book I told you, Theophilus, about
everything Jesus began to do and teach.
Acts 1:1 NLT

Luke was the traveling companion of the Apostle Paul. He joined Paul on his 2ⁿᵈ and 3ʳᵈ missionary journeys, Acts 20. Luke was a Gentile by birth, well educated in Greek customs, a beloved physician by profession, a companion of Paul at various times, even until his final imprisonment in Rome. According to 2 Timothy 4:11, Luke remained with the Apostle Paul after others had deserted him.

The Gospel of Luke has 24 chapters. In these chapters, Luke presents Jesus as our compassionate Savior showing love and kindness to all people, especially, the poor, oppressed, the women, and the outcast of society.

Note of Interests: Matthew presents Jesus to be the promised Jewish Messiah; Mark shows Jesus to be the Servant of God and John emphasizes Jesus' deity and identified him as the Son of God.

~~~~~~~~~~~~

Luke presents the importance of understanding the way of salvation in the works and teaching of Jesus. He emphasizes divine mercy which was illustrated in Luke 7, the raising of the widow of Nain's son raised from the dead, and the prodigal son who returns to his father and asked forgiveness, Luke 15.

Note of Interests: Jesus raising the son of the widow of Nain is the 1st of 3 miracles in which Jesus raised the dead. The other two are Jarius' the synagogue ruler's daughter, and Mary and Martha's brother Lazarus; Mark 5 and John 11.

~~~~~~~~~~~~

The Gospel of Luke's account of Jesus' ministry can be divided into 4 main events:

1. The beginning events of John the Baptist and Jesus, Chapter 1:1 – 4:13.
2. The events that occurred in and around Galilee, Chapters 4:14 – 9:50.
3. The events that took place in Judea and Perea, Chapters 9:51 – 19:27.
4. The events in the final week in Jerusalem, Chapters 19:28 – 24:53.

The 11th chapter of Luke can be outlined as follows:

I.   The Lord's Prayer, vs. 1 – 4
II.   Perseverance in Prayer, vs. 5 – 13
III. Jesus and the Prince of Demons, vs. 14 – 23
IV.   The Return of the Unclean Evil Spirit, vs. 24 – 26
V.   True Blessedness, vs. 27 - 28
VI.   Evil Generation Asked for a Miraculous Sign, vs. 29 – 32
VII. The Lamp is the Eye of the Body, vs. 33 – 36
VIII. Jesus Denounces Pharisees and Lawyers, vs. 37 – 54

The 29th verse of Luke 11 reads:

As the crowd pressed in on Jesus, he said, "This evil generation keeps asking me to show them miraculous sign. But the only sign I will give them is the sign of Jonah. NLT

Why did Jesus call this crowd "a wicked generation?" Jesus had just performed a miracle before the crowd. He had cast out a demon in a mute man, which prevented him from speaking. Some of the people in the crowd accused Jesus of casting out the mute spirit by Beelzebul, the prince of the demons, Luke 11:15.

Afterward, Jesus made the following statement and asked a question, "Any kingdom divided against itself will be ruined, and a house divided against itself will fall. If Satan is divided against himself, how can his kingdom stand," Luke 11:18 – 19?

When the people in the crowd refused to acknowledge the miracle that had just happened before their eyes, Jesus called them "a wicked generation." Jesus told the unbelievers in the crowd that he wouldn't give them a sign from heaven to prove that he wasn't exercising His power by the prince of demons. Jesus said the only sign that will be given to them is the sign of Jonah. In comparison, Jonah the prophet was in the fish belly for 3 days, and Jesus will be in the earth for 3 days, after his death and burial.

Chapter 16

JOHN 11:29

**As soon as she heard that, she arose
quickly, and came unto him.**
John 11:29 KJV

~~~

The Apostle John, the brother of James, the son of Zebedee, one of the 12 disciples, and the disciple whom Jesus loved, is the writer of the Gospel of John, John 13:23. He was a prominent leader in the early development of the Christian church.

The Gospel of John is about Jesus' life is the last of the 4 gospels in the New Testament. John states the purpose of his gospel is "that ye might believe that Jesus is the Christ, the Son of God; and that believing ye might have life through his name," John 20:31, KJV.

John's Gospel focuses on a new life in Jesus. The other gospels focus on "The Kingdom of God" and "The Kingdom of Heaven." It's from John's Gospel that we get Jesus cherished statement, "I am the way and the truth and the life. No man comes to the Father except through me," John 14:6.

John's Gospel is different than the other 3 in several ways.

1. John begins with the unique and profound announcement that Jesus is "In the beginning," John 1:1.
2. John's Gospel is a witness for the people who weren't there to see Jesus or his ministry.
3. John concentrate on Jesus the Christ; not his miracles.
4. John mentioned more of Jesus' dialogues. Jesus words to Nicodemus, John 3:16; The Samaritan Woman, John 4:4-26; The Man at the Pool, John 5:1-9;
   The Woman Taken in Adultery, John 7:53 -8:11, Jesus conversation with Marth and Mary, John 11:17-33, etc.
5. The word "life" appears 38 times in John's Gospel, more than the others.
6. John's Gospel records the most metaphors from Jesus, John 6:35, John 8:12, John 10:7, John 10:11, John 11:25, John 14:6, John 15:1 and John 15:5. A few examples are listed below:

John 6:35

And Jesus said unto them, I am the bread of life: he that cometh to me shall never hunger; and then he that believe on me shall never thirst.

John 11:25

Jesus said unto her, I am the resurrection, and the life: he that believeth in me, though he was dead, yet shall he live.

John 15:5

I am the vine, ye are the branches: He that abideth in me, and I in him, the same bringeth forth much fruit: for without me ye can do nothing.

A brief outline of John 11 is as follows:

    I.   The Death of Lazarus, vs. 1 – 16
    II. Jesus Comforts Lazarus' Sisters, vs. 17 – 27
    III. Jesus Weeps, vs. 28 – 37
    IV. Jesus Raises Lazarus from the Dead, vs. 38 – 44
    V. The Jewish Leaders Plot to Kill Jesus, vs. 45 – 57

The 29th verse of John 11 is surrounding the section titled Jesus Weeps. It reads is as follows: When Mary heard this, she got up quickly and went to him. NIV

When Martha heard that Jesus was coming into town, she went out to greet him, but Mary stayed home. Mary was setting in the house with many Jews who were there to comfort her and her sister because of the death of their brother; this was the Jewish customs, John 11:19 – 20.

Martha said to Jesus, "Lord if you had been here, my brother wouldn't have died." Jesus said, "Your brother will rise again." Martha answered, "I know he will rise again at the time of the resurrection." Jesus said to her, "I am the resurrection. I am life." Martha tells Jesus she believes he is the Messiah, the Son of God.

Martha went back to the house and in private told Mary that the Teacher is asking for her. Mary sprang up from her attitude of mourning and grief and went to meet the True Comforter, Jesus.

Note of Interests: In John 11, Jesus raised Lazarus from the dead; this was Jesus 7th and last miracle in the Book of John. The other miracles are as follows:

1. Jesus Turns Water to Wine, John 2:1-11.
2. Jesus Heals the Official's Son, John 4:43-54.
3. Jesus Heals the Man at the Pool of Bethesda, John 5:1-9
4. Jesus Fed 5000 with 5 Loaves of Bread & 2 Fish, John 6:1-5
5. Jesus Walks on Water, John 6:16-25
6. Jesus Heals the Man Born Blind, John 9:1-41

~~~~~~~~~~~~

The Acts of the Apostles

Chapter 17

ACTS 11:29

Then the disciples, every man according to his ability, determined to send relief unto the brethren which dwelt in Judaea:
Acts 11:29 KJV

~ ~ ~

The book titled <u>Acts of the Apostles</u> is the 5th book in the New Testament. This book is also referred to as "Acts" and the "Book of Acts," and it's addressed to the same individual as the Book of Luke which was Theophilus. It describes the early days of the Christian's ministry and how it spread throughout the Roman Empire.

Note of Interests: The New Testament refers to Caesar Augustus as the emperor during the time of Jesus' birth, Luke 2. He came to power in 31 BC during a time of widespread dissatisfaction with the current government following the murder of Julius Caesar. The population of the Roman Empire at that time was near 85,000,000. The boundaries of the Roman Empire consisted of the British Channel, the Rhine, the Danube, and the Black Sea on the north; the deserts of Africa, the waterfall of the Nile, and the Arabian deserts on the south; the Euphrates River on the east; and the Atlantic Ocean on the west.

~~~~~~~~~~~~

The Gospel of Luke and the Acts of the Apostles make up a two-volume work which biblical scholars call "Luke–Acts." They were written between 80 – 90 AD by Luke and accounts for 27.5% of the New Testament. The Acts of the Apostles have 28 chapters, and the Gospel of Luke has 24.

The Gospel of Luke recorded how God fulfilled his plan for the world's salvation through Jesus' life, death, and resurrection. The Acts of the Apostles continues the events that surround Christianity in the 1st century, beginning with Jesus' ascension to heaven.

Jesus provided the promised salvation to the Jews in the Gospels, and in Acts, it was extended to the Gentiles. Apostles Peter and Paul are two significant individuals in the Acts of the Apostles.

The Acts of the Apostles has 4 major divisions:

I. **Peter and the Church in Jerusalem, Chapters 1 – 7**

The 1st division in Acts is the coming of the Holy Spirit at Pentecost, the birth of the Christian church. Throughout these chapters, Luke narrates how the church prayed, fellowshipped, shared meals and even their goods. The Apostles boldly preached the Gospel and performed many signs and wonders. The religious leaders of the

Jews immediately began a campaign of persecution. They demanded the Apostles to cease preaching in the name of Christ. This persecution utterly led to the stoning of Stephen, the church's first martyr.

II. <u>The Church in Judea and Samaria, Chapters 8 – 12</u>

In these chapters, when persecution broke-out in Jerusalem, the disciples spread to other parts of Israel, and some went as far as Antioch. According to Acts 8, Phillip preaches the Gospel in Samaria. The conversion of the Ethiopian eunuch and Cornelius occurred in Acts 8 and 10. Cornelius then helped spread the Gospel to the Gentiles. The transformation of Saul's (Paul) on the road to Damascus happened in Acts 9. Paul becomes the leading individual in Chapters 13 – 28 of Acts.

III. <u>Paul and the Church in Gentile Territories, Chapters 13 – 20</u>

These chapters take the Gospel into Gentile territories. The man responsible for this is the Apostle Paul. Luke narrates 3 separate missionary journeys which took Paul through the regions of Galatia, Europe (Philippi, Thessalonica, Corinth) and Asia Minor (Ephesus). In chapter 15, Luke gives an account of the Jerusalem Council. They redefined the concept of the people of God. The Gentiles Christians were officially accepted and united into God's covenant.

IV. **Paul's Trials and Voyage to Rome, Chapters 21 – 28**

In the final section of Acts, Paul is in a legal battle against his adversaries. He journeys to Rome to appeal his case before Caesar. Paul is a prisoner, and he is no longer planting churches for Christ Jesus but instead defending himself before Roman governors. The Book of Acts ends with Paul's final appeals to his Jewish countrymen to accept Jesus as their Messiah.

The section titled The Church in Judea and Samaria is where Acts 11:29 is located. The NLT verse reads as follows, "So, the believers in Antioch decided to send relief to the brothers and sisters in Judea, everyone giving as much as they could."

When the Prophet Agabus along with others from Antioch traveled to Jerusalem. He was shown by the power of the Spirit, that a severe famine would sweep across the Roman empire. It was in the 4th year of Emperor Claudius Caesar when this famine began and lasted for several years. During this time, thousands of people died from starvation.

According to Acts 11:29, "the disciples, each according to his ability, decided to send relief to the brothers living in Judea." The Gentile Church in Antioch sends gifts to the Jewish Church of Jerusalem by Barnabas and Saul as a provision for the famine; this was the 1st example of Christian love that was encouraged by Paul throughout his ministry. Helping others, the poor and the needy became one of the missions of the Apostles' ministry, Acts 24:17, Romans 15:25-26, 1 Corinthians 16:1, Galatians 2:10.

The Pauline Epistles

Romans
1 Corinthians
2 Corinthians
Galatians
Ephesians
Philippians
Colossians
1 Thessalonians
2 Thessalonians
1 Timothy
2 Timothy
Titus
Philemon

Only Romans, 1 Corinthians, 2 Corinthians have an 11th chapter with a 29th verse.

There are 13 Pauline Epistles which are also called "Epistles of Paul" and "Letters of Paul." The name "Paul" is the first word of each letter. The New Testament consists of 27 books, and Paul the Apostle wrote 13.

Chapter 18

ROMANS 11:29

**For the gifts and calling of God
are without repentance.**
Romans 11:29 KJV

~ ~ ~

The Book of Romans has 16 chapters. It provides information on topics such as judgment, spiritual growth, salvation by grace, faith in Jesus, the righteousness and sovereignty of God.

Romans chapters 1 – 8, Paul explains the fundamentals and foundations of the Christian faith with believers and tells them they are commanded to share this with the world. In Chapters 9 – 11, Paul describes God's sovereignty over salvation. He explains how an individual comes into right relationship with God. In chapters 12 – 16, Paul gives instructions on how Christians are to live a holy life.

Biblical scholars believe the Book of Romans was written in the early spring of 57 AD. It is believed that Paul was on his 3rd missionary journey. He was returning to Jerusalem with the offering from the mission churches for the poverty-stricken believers in Jerusalem, Romans 15:25 – 27. Scholars believe that Phoebe delivered the letter to the Christian believers in Rome. Therefore, it is also called "The Epistle to the Romans" or "Letter to the Romans," and "Romans" for short.

Note of Interests: Phoebe was a 1ˢᵗ-century Christian woman. She was a notable woman in the church of Cenchrea about 8 miles east of Corinth. Paul trusted her to deliver his letter to the Romans. He refers to her as a deaconess and as a patron of many. Romans is the only book in the New Testament where a woman is mentioned with two worthy honors.

~~~~~~~~~~~~

The 11ᵗʰ chapter of Romans is about:

I.   The Remnant of Israel, vs.1 – 10
II. Gentiles Grafted In, 11 – 24
III. Israel's Salvation, vs. 25 – 32
IV. Praise to God, vs. 33 – 36

The 29ᵗʰ verse falls under the title <u>Israel's Salvation</u>. The 29ᵗʰ verse is the end of the 28ᵗʰ verse. The complete verse reads as follows:

<u>**Romans 11:28 – 29 NIV**</u>

28. As far as the gospel is concerned, they are enemies for your sake; but as far as election is concerned, they are loved on account of the patriarchs, 29. For God's gifts and his call are irrevocable.

<u>Romans 11:28 – 29 NLT</u>

28. Many of the people Israel are now enemies of the Good News, and this benefits you Gentiles. Yet they are still the people he loves because he chose their ancestors Abraham, Isaac, and Jacob. 29. For God's gifts and his call can never be withdrawn.

The NLT (New Living Translation) helps provides a little more understanding on this verse. The Apostle Paul is announcing that the purposes of God are unchangeable, and His gifts and callings irrevocable. What God has promised Israel He will not withdraw. The fact that Israel is His special people will never change. God will never revoke the gifts that He has bestowed upon Israel. For example, when Jerusalem was destroyed the Jewish nation wasn't exterminated. The kingdom of Israel cannot be deprived of what God promised to do with and for them.

Chapter 19

1 CORINTHIANS 11:29

**For he that eateth and drinketh unworthily,
eateth and drinketh damnation to himself,
not discerning the Lord's body.**
1 Corinthians 11:29 KJV

~~~

The city of Corinth was the chief city of Greece when Paul visited it. It was considered one of the most wicked cities of Paul's times. The population during Paul's visit was about 400,000 which consists of Greeks, Jews, Italians, refugees from all over the world and a mixed multitude from everywhere. The people brought with them their beliefs, religions, and gods.

The church of Corinth was founded by Paul on his 2nd missionary journey, Acts 18. While Paul was there, he stayed with Aquila and Priscilla. They were Jews who had been expelled from Rome and were members of the church, Acts 18:2 – 3 The church of Corinth was far from the perfect church. There had been many recent converts to Christianity, and some of their heathen customs and practices were being allowed in the church. The household

Vanessa Rayner

of Chloe sent a message to Paul informing him about the severe quarrels and problems that were taking place among the Christians at Corinth.

First and Second Corinthians are full of information concerning the many problems the church faced. First Corinthians contains 16 chapters, and Second Corinthians has 13. First Corinthians was written from the city of Ephesus before Pentecost in the late spring, 1 Corinthians 16:5 – 8.

The Book of 1ˢᵗ Corinthians can be outlined as follows:

1.	Salutation and Thanksgiving	Chapter 1:1 – 9
2.	Divisions:	Chapters 1 thru 4
	Facts of division	
	Causes of division	
	Cures for division	
3.	Correction of Moral Disorders	Chapters 5 and 6
	Discipline an immoral brother	
	Resolving personal disputes	
	Sexual purity	
4.	Paul's Answers to Questions	Chapters 7
	Marriage	thru 14
	Christian liberty Worship	
	Lord's Supper	
5.	The Doctrine of Resurrection	Chapter 15
6.	Closing	Chapter 16

Remember, 1ˢᵗ Corinthians is a corrective and instructive letter from Paul to the church in Corinth. One of the many issues Apostle Paul addressed is the manner in which the people were taking communion; the Lord's Supper.

When Paul heard what the people were doing at communion, 1st Corinthians 11:29 was one of the statements he made. The NLT reads as follows, "For it you eat the bread or drink the cup without honouring the body of Christ, you are eating and drinking God's judgment upon yourself."

In brief, the people were not treating communion as a sacred ordinance instituted by Jesus. Instead of the people remembering Jesus' sacrifice, communion became a time of self-indulgence. Others were rushing to eat their meal without sharing with others. Some Christians were left hungry; and then others were getting drunk, disgracing God's church, verses 20 – 22.

Paul asked the people to examine themselves before communion. He asked them were they eating the meal to remember Christ's sacrifice or are they just satisfying their appetites?

Paul explained, how to honor the body of Christ at communion by reflecting on Jesus' sacrifice to the world. The Lord's Supper is a time to look within and confess our sins. The Lord's Supper should be conducted with joy, reverence, and honesty. Paul then states the consequence for not honoring the body of Christ, 1 Corinthians 11:29.

1 Corinthians 11:29 NIV

For those who eat and drink without discerning the body of Christ eat and drink judgement on themselves.

Chapter 20

2 CORINTHIANS 11:29

Who is weak, and I am not weak? Who is offended, and I burn not?
2 Corinthians 11:29 KJV

~~~

The 2ⁿᵈ Epistle to the Corinthians have 13 chapters, and it is often referred to as 2 Corinthians or the Book of 2ⁿᵈ Corinthians. It is one of the Pauline Epistles, a letter from Apostle Paul to the church at Corinth and Christians throughout Achaia, 2 Corinthians 1:1. Second Corinthians was given to Titus to hand-deliver to the church, 2 Corinthians 8:6.

Second Corinthians is the 8ᵗʰ book in the New Testament and was written around 56 AD. It's believed that 1 Corinthians and 2 Corinthians were written the same year, but 2 Corinthians were written later that year before the arrival of winter from the city of Macedonia.

Note of Interests: Scholars believe Paul wrote at least 4 letters to the church of Corinth because of references made within 1 and 2 Corinthians. The first reference is made at

1 Corinthians 5:9, Paul refers to as a "former letter." The second reference is made at 2 Corinthians 2:3 – 4, Paul refers to as a "sorrowful letter." Those two letters are viewed as lost or unfound, at this time.

~~~~~~~~~~~~

Paul wrote the Book of 2nd Corinthians to the church in Corinth to defend and protect his Apostleship and to teach and warn against false teachers who were spreading heresy. The last thing Apostle Paul explains in 2 Corinthians is how to test yourself. If you want to know if you are a Christian, a believer and follower of Jesus Christ, you must examine yourself with Scripture, "to see if you are in the faith," 2 Corinthians 13:5.

The Book of 2nd Corinthians can be outlined as follows:

Paul's Explains His Ministry, Chapters 1 – 7

Paul explained that his ministry was to preach Jesus Christ, "For we do not preach ourselves, but Christ Jesus as Lord, and ourselves as bondservants for Jesus' sake," 2 Corinthians 4:5. Paul explains that Christians will suffer but compared to eternity with Christ the sufferings of this world are temporary and have a purpose for us.

Christians Given to the Christians at Jerusalem, Chapters 8 – 9

Paul urges the Corinthians to give an offering to the believers in Judea. He stressed if they give generously they would also "reap generously," 2 Corinthians 9:6.

Apostle Paul Defends His Calling, Chapters 10 – 13

Paul defends his ministry and responds to those opposing him and attacking his Apostleship. He speaks about his sufferings. Paul makes it clear, if anyone preaches a different Gospel or a different Jesus, other than what he and the Apostles were preaching, they are false teachers and should not be accepted.

The 11th chapter of 2 Corinthians can be divided into two sections.

1. Paul and the False Apostles, vs. 1 – 15
2. Paul Suffering for Christ, vs. 16 – 33

The 29th verse reads as follows:

NIV

Who is weak, and I do not feel weak? Who is led into sin, and I do not inwardly burn?

<u>NLT</u>

Who is weak without my feeling that weakness? Who is led astray, and I do not burn with anger?

This verse is among the section titled <u>Paul's Suffering for Christ</u>. The Apostle Paul is defending his ministry and Apostleship. His defense started in 2 Corinthians 10 and carried into chapter 13.

However, in chapter 11 Paul mentioned the trials, tribulations, and suffering he had gone through for being an Apostle for Christ Jesus. Beginning at verse 23, Paul states he has worked hard, and faced death over and over, for being a servant of Christ.

Paul then tells the people what he has suffered.

1. 5 times the Jewish leaders gave him 39 lashes
2. 3 times he was beaten with rods
3. 1 times he stoned to near death
4. 3 times he was shipwrecked and spent 1 night and a day adrift at sea
5. He traveled on many long journeys, faced danger from robbers
6. He faced threats from his people, the Jews, as well as the Gentiles
7. He met danger in the cities, the deserts, and on the seas
8. He faced threats from men who claim to be believers but weren't

9. He worked hard and long, enduring many sleepless nights
10. He has been hungry and thirsty, and many times went without food
11. He shivered in the cold without enough clothing to keep him warm
12. Besides all this, he had the daily burden of concern for all the churches

After Paul states what he has suffered through, he asked a question which is verse 29, "Who is weak without my feeling that weakness? Who is led astray, and I do not burn with anger?"

In the first part of this verse, Paul is saying, whoever is weak in the faith he is concerned for them. He immediately wants to restore and strengthen them, again. When they experience stressful, heart-breaking, disappointing circumstances, he feels what they feel, and is affected by the situation.

In the second part of this verse, Paul is saying, he hasn't scandalized or cause anyone to stumble and fall. When an individual is led astray by false prophets, he burns with zeal to restore that person, and with anger against the tempter.

Note of Interests: The next book in the Bible that have an 11th chapter is Hebrews. The following books that are between 2 Corinthians and Hebrews have less than 11 chapters:

1. Galatians (6)
2. Ephesians (6)   Prison Epistle

3.	Philippians (4)	Prison Epistle
4.	Colossians (4)	Prison Epistle
5.	1 Thessalonians (5)	
6.	2 Thessalonians (3)	
7.	1 Timothy (6)	Pastoral Epistle
8.	2 Timothy (4)	Pastoral Epistle
9.	Titus (3)	Pastoral Epistle
10.	Philemon (1)	Prison Epistle

Apostle Paul wrote the Prison and Pastoral Epistles while he was in prison. The Prison Epistles were delivered to the churches, and a slave owner named Philemon by his disciples. The Pastoral Epistles were letters with instructions for pastors concerning the church organization, discipline and general functions within the church. Paul wrote 1 Timothy to encourage Timothy concerning the Ephesian church. Paul 2nd letter to Timothy was written around 67 AD, shortly before Apostle Paul was put to death by the orders of the emperor Nero in Rome. The 2nd letter to Timothy is considered Paul last words; to persevere in faith, and proclaim the gospel of Jesus Christ to all, 2 Timothy 3:14 and 2 Timothy 4:2.

~~~~~~~~~~~~

Chapter 21

HEBREWS 11:29

**By faith they passed through the
Red Sea as by dry land:
which the Egyptians assaying to do were drowned.**
Hebrews 11:29 KJV

~ ~ ~

The Epistle of Hebrews boldly proclaims the superiority of Jesus Christ. It was written before the destruction of the Temple in 70 AD. The Book of Hebrews opens with the triumph of Jesus as "the brightness of God's glory and the express image of His being, and upholding all things by His powerful word," Hebrews 1:3. Jesus is presented as the "captain," "forerunner," "Son of God," "high priest," and "great high priest" in the Book of Hebrews.

The Epistle of the Hebrews is also called the "Book of Hebrews." It is the 19th book in the New Testament; 58th book in the Bible. The Book of Hebrews has 13 chapters, contains 303 verses and approximately 6,900 words; this book is considered a "masterpiece" by scholars. It was written to the Hebrew Christians who were wavering in their faith. Although addressed to Hebrew Christians this book speaks to everyone.

The author of Hebrews doesn't name himself, but the Apostle Paul has been suggested as the author by scholars. Others believe Priscilla's wrote Hebrews, but her name was taken out to prevent ridicule of the book. There are those who suggest that Barnabas, Luke, Clement of Rome and Apollos could be the writer. The Book of Hebrews also explains practical instructions for following Jesus; being his disciple.

Important words in the Epistle of Hebrews are better (12), mediator (6), sacrifice (17), and faith (34); Romans also mention faith 34 times, KJV. Even though, the word "mediator" is only mentioned in the Bible 6 times; 3 of those 6 times are in Hebrews.

*Jesus is better. Jesus Christ, the Son of God, is better than angels, priests, leaders of the Old Testament (Moses, Joshua, Aaron, David, etc.), or any religion (Judaism, Pharisees, Sadducees, Essenes, etc.), Hebrews 1:4. When Jesus died on the cross of Calvary and rose from the grave on the 3rd day, He paid the price for believers' salvation.

*Jesus is our mediator. Jesus Christ is our only mediator between God and man, 1 Timothy 2:5, Hebrews 8:6. The promise of salvation was fulfilled through the sacrifice of God's Son, Jesus Christ.

*Jesus Christ is our sacrifice. The Old Testament's laws, rituals, and animal sacrifices pointed toward Jesus. When we received Jesus Christ as our Savior, our sins are forgiven.

*Faith pleases God. Faith is expressed by obeying God. According to Hebrews 11:6, "But without faith, it is impossible to please God."

A simple outline of the Book of Hebrews is as follows:

1. Jesus Christ is Superior to Angels -   Hebrews 1:1 – 2:18
2. Jesus is Superior to the Law -   Hebrews 3:1 – 10:18
3. A Call to Endure through Trials -   Hebrews 10:19 – 12:29
4. Final Exhortations and Greetings -   Hebrews 13:1 – 25

There are approximately 100 Old Testament references in the Book of Hebrews. The books of Exodus and Leviticus are very beneficial in understanding Hebrews.

Chapter 11 of the Book of Hebrews list a host of Old Testament individuals who did "Acts Prompted by Faith." The 1st verse of chapter 11 describes "faith."

Now faith is being sure of what we hope
for and certain of what we do not see.
Hebrews 11:1 NIV

The 29th verse of Hebrews 11 is part of the "Acts Prompted by Faith."

Vs. 3   By faith we understand God's words created the universe

Vs. 4   By faith Abel offered a better sacrifice to God than Cain

Vs. 5   By faith Enoch didn't see death; God took him up

Vs. 7   By faith Noah built an ark

Vs. 8   By faith Abraham traveled to an unknown land

Vs. 9   By faith Abraham lived as a stranger in an area he was promised

Vs. 10   By faith Sarah birthed a promised child in her old age

Vs. 17   By faith Abraham offered Isaac when he was tested

Vs. 20   By faith Isaac blessed Jacob and Esau concerning the future

Vs. 21   By faith Jacob blessed each of Joseph's sons on his dying bed

Vs. 22   By faith Joseph gave instruction where to bury his bones

Vs. 23   By faith Moses parents hid him for 3 months when he was born

Vs. 24   By faith Moses refused to be called the son of Pharaoh's daughter

Vs. 27   By faith Israel left Egypt

Vs. 28   By faith Israel kept the Passover and the sprinkling of blood

Vs. 29 **It was by faith that the people of Israel went right through the Red Sea as though they were on dry ground. But when the Egyptians tried to follow, they were all drowned. NLT**

Vs. 30 By faith Jericho's walls fell

Vs. 31 By faith Rahab the prostitute hid the Israelite spies

Note of Interests: The books in the Bible that is after the Book of Hebrews, and don't have an 11th chapter are James (5), 1 Peter (5), 2 Peter (3), 1 John (5), 2 John (1), 3 John (1), and Jude (1). Revelation is the last book of the New Testament. It has 22 chapters, but the 11th chapter only has 19 verses.

~~~~~~~~~~~~

A Reader's Question

This new section just dropped in my spirit at 0613 on January 14, 2017, titled <u>A Reader's Question.</u>

An individual asked me the following question:
"Will I be doing more publicity this year?"

<u>The Answer</u>:
I don't think so, at this time.
I will continue to pray, fast, and seek Father's guidance.

**In all thy ways acknowledge him,
and He shall direct thy paths.**
Proverbs 3:6

Author's Closing Remarks

Glory be to God! . . . . I'm dreaming 11:29. . . *How about you? smile*

Which Biblical Event will **YOU** remember *from this moment on,* when you see 11:29 on a mailbox, work clock, house address, on a vehicle tag, your watch, someone birthday, price on an item, and the list goes on.

11:29

Now, check the Biblical Events which surrounds 11:29 that you remember. I pray all 19, but the majority is good too.

____1. Genesis 11:29　　　　____2. Leviticus 11:29

____3. Numbers 11:29　　　　____4. Deuteronomy 11:29

____5. Judges 11:29　　　　　____6. 1 Kings 11:29

____7. 1 Chronicles 11:29　　____8. Nehemiah 11:29

____9. Proverbs 11:29　　　　____10. Daniel 11:29

____11. Matthew 11:29　　　　____12. Mark 11:29

____13. Luke 11:29　　　　　 ____14. John 11:29

____15. Acts 11:29　　　　　 ____16. Romans 11:29

____17. 1 Corinthians 11:29 ____18. 2 Corinthians 11:29

____19. Hebrews 11:29

P.S.: In the back of the book, a list of the verses is together. Strive to study them until you know all 19 by heart. Be Bless in Jesus' Name, you feel the difference, experience the strength, and see His power.

Pray for the Ministry . . . *May the "LORD of Peace," give you His Peace.*

Dr. Vanessa

References

Chapter 1   Numbered Verses
    1.   <u>Isaiah 26:3-4 "Perfect Peace" The Last Single Digit</u> by Vanessa Buckhalter

Chapter 2   11th chapter, 29th verse
    1.   BibleGateway: <u>https://www.biblegateway.com</u>

Chapter 3   Genesis 11:29
    1.   BibleGateway: <u>https://www.biblegateway.com</u>
    2.   Wikipedia, The Free Encyclopedia: <u>https://en.wikipedia.org/wiki/Book_of_Genesis</u>

Chapter 4   Leviticus 11:29
    1.   Jacksonville Theological Seminary
    2.   Wikipedia, The Free Encyclopedia: <u>https://en.wikipedia.org/wiki/Book_of_Leviticus</u>
    3.   BibleGateway: <u>https://www.biblegateway.com</u>

Chapter 5   Numbers 11:29
    1.   Wikipedia, The Free Encyclopedia: <u>https://en.wikipedia.org/wiki/Book_of_Numbers</u>
    2.   BibleHub: <u>https://biblehub.com/summary/number/1.htm</u>

Chapter 6   Deuteronomy 11:29
    1.   Wikipedia, The Free Encyclopedia: <u>https://en.wikipedia.org/wiki/Tanakh</u>

2. Wikipedia, The Free Encyclopedia: https://en.wikipedia.org/wiki/Book_of_Deuteronomy

Chapter 7   Judges 11:29
1. Wikipedia, The Free Encyclopedia: https://en.wikipedia.org/wiki/Book_of_Judges
2. BibleGateway: https://www.biblegateway.com

Chapter 8   1 Kings 11:29
1. BibleGateway: https://www.biblegateway.com
2. Wikipedia, The Free Encyclopedia: https://en.wikipedia.org/wiki/Book_of_First_Kings

Chapter 9   1 Chronicles 11:29
1. BibleGateway: https://www.biblegateway.com
2. Wikipedia, The Free Encyclopedia: https://en.wikipedia.org/wiki/Book_of_First_Chronicles

Chapter 10   Nehemiah 11:29
1. Wikipedia, The Free Encyclopedia: https://en.wikipedia.org/wiki/Book_of_Nehemiah
1. BibleGateway: https://www.biblegateway.com

Chapter 11   Proverbs 11:29
1. BibleGateway: https://www.biblegateway.com
2. Jacksonville Theology Seminary

Chapter 12   Daniel 11:29
1. BibleGateway: https://www.biblegateway.com
2. Wikipedia, The Free Encyclopedia: https://en.wikipedia.org/wiki/Book_of_Daniel

Chapter 13   Matthew 11:29
    1.   BibleGateway: https://www.biblegateway.com
    2.   Jacksonville Theology Seminary

Chapter 14   Mark 11:29
    1.   BibleGateway: https://www.biblegateway.com
    2.   Jacksonville Theology Seminary

Chapter 15   Luke 11:29
    1.   BibleGateway: https://www.biblegateway.com
    2.   Jacksonville Theology Seminary

Chapter 16   John 11:29
    1.   BibleGateway: https://www.biblegateway.com
    2.   Jacksonville Theology Seminary

Chapter 17   Acts 11:29
    1.   BibleGateway: https://www.biblegateway.com
    2.   Jacksonville Theology Seminary

Chapter 18   Romans 11:29
    1.   BibleGateway: https://www.biblegateway.com
    2.   Biblehub: https://www.biblehub.com/summary/romans/1.htm

Chapter 19   1 Corinthians 11:29
    1.   Wikipedia, The Free Encyclopedia: https://www.enwikipedia.org/wiki/First_Epistle_to_the_Corinthians
    2.   BibleGateway: https://www.biblegateway.com

Chapter 20   2 Corinthians 11:29

    1. Bible Study Tools: https://www.biblestudytools.com/2-corinthians

    2. BibleGateway: https://www.biblegateway.com

Chapter 21   Hebrews 11:29

    1. BibleGateway: https://www.biblegateway.com

    2. Wikipedia, The Free Encyclopedia: https://en.wikipedia.org/wiki/Book_of_Hebrews

Answers & Information Section

Chapter 9   1 Chronicles 11:29
The Northern Tribes of Israel

1.   Asher
2.   Dan
3.   Gad
4.   Issachar
5.   Ephraim   (Joseph's son)
6.   Manasseh   (Joseph's son)
7.   Naphtali
8.   Reuben
9.   Simeon
10. Zebulun

Regina (Sister) Vanessa Dalshundria (Niece)

Other Books by the Author:

From the Pew to the Pulpit	Published: 08/29/2007
Isaiah 26:3-4 "Perfect Peace"	Published: 09/07/2010
Isaiah 26:3-4 "Perfect Peace" The Last Single Digit	Published: 02/13/2012
Isaiah 26:3-4 "Perfect Peace III" Silver and Gold	Published: 10/24/2012
Isaiah 26:3-4 "Perfect Peace IV" The Kingdom Number	Published: 04/10/2013
Isaiah 26:3-4 "Perfect Peace V" 2541	Published: 09/06/2013
Isaiah 26:3-4 "Perfect Peace VI" Zacchaeus	Published: 02/28/2014
Isaiah 26:3-4 "Perfect Peace VII" Eleven	Published: 10/29/2014
Isaiah 26:3-4 "Perfect Peace VIII" Prayer	Published: 05/22/2015
Isaiah 26:3-4 "Perfect Peace IX" Sixteen	Published: 10/26/2015
Isaiah 26:3-4 "Perfect Peace X" Dreams	Published: 04/12/2016
Isaiah 26:3-4 "Perfect Peace XI" Door	Published: 02/13/2017

The 11:29 List

And Abram and Nahor took them wives: the name of Abram's wife was Sarai; and the name of Nahor's wife, Milcah, the daughter of Haran, the father of Milcah, and the father of Iscah. Genesis 11:29 KJV

~~~

These also shall be unclean unto you among the creeping things that creep upon the earth; the weasel, and the mouse, and the tortoise after his kind. Leviticus 11:29 KJV

~~~

And Moses said unto him, Enviest thou for my sake? would God that all the Lord's people were prophets, and that the Lord would put his spirit upon them! Numbers 11:29 KJV

~~~

And it shall come to pass, when the Lord they God hath brought thee in unto the land whither thou goest to possess it, that thou shalt put the blessing upon mount Gerizim, and the curse upon mount Ebal. Deuteronomy 11:29 KJV

~~~

Then the Spirit of the Lord came upon Jephthah, and he passed over Gilead, and Manasseh, and passed over Mizpeh of Gilead, and from Mizpeh of Gilead he passed over unto the children of Ammon. Judges 11:29 KJV

~~~

And it came to pass at that time when Jeroboam went out of Jerusalem, that the prophet Ahijah the Shilonite found him in the way; and he had clad himself with a new garment; and they two were alone in the field: 1 Kings 11:29 KJV

~~~

Sibbecai the Hushathite, Ilai the Ahohite, 1 Chronicles 11:29 KJV

~~~

And at Enrimmon, and at Zareah, and at Jarmuth, Nehemiah 11:29 KJV

~~~

He that troubleth his own house shall inherit the wind: and the fool shall be servant to the wise of heart. Proverbs 11:29 KJV

~~~

At the time appointed he shall return, and come toward the south; but it shall not be as the former, or as the latter. Daniel 11:29 KJV

~~~

Take my yoke upon you, and learn of me; for I am meek and lowly in heart: and ye shall find rest unto your souls. Matthew 11:29 KJV

~~~

And Jesus answered and said unto them, I will also ask of you one question, and answer me, and I will tell you by what authority I do these things. Mark 11:29 KJV

~~~

And when the people were gathered thick together, he began to say, This is an evil generation: they seek a sign; and there shall no sign be given it, but the sign of Jonas the prophet. Luke 11:29 KJV

~~~

As soon as she heard that, she arose quickly, and came unto him. John 11:29 KJV

~~~

Then the disciples, every man according to his ability, determined to send relief unto the brethren which dwelt in Judaea: Acts 11:29 KJV

~~~

For the gifts and calling of God are without repentance. Romans 11:29 KJV

~~~

For he that eateth and drinketh unworthily, eateth and drinketh damnation to himself, not discerning the Lord's body. 1 Corinthians 11:29 KJV

~~~

Who is weak, and I am not weak? Who is offended, and I burn not? 2 Corinthians 11:29 KJV

~~~

By faith they passed through the Red Sea as by dry land: which the Egyptians assaying to do were drowned. Hebrews 11:29 KJV

~~~